101 Inspirational Coloring Mandalas
COLORING BOOK
Currated by Todd Cotton

---

*"No matter how much we grow taller, grow older,
we are still forever stumbling...forever wondering, forever young.*

This publication is part of a series of products and publications.
For more information, please visit: **http://www.101bookclub.com.**

"101 Book Club" is a subsidiary of
Top of the Nation Enterprises, Inc.

"If you can dream it, you can do it."
Walt Disney

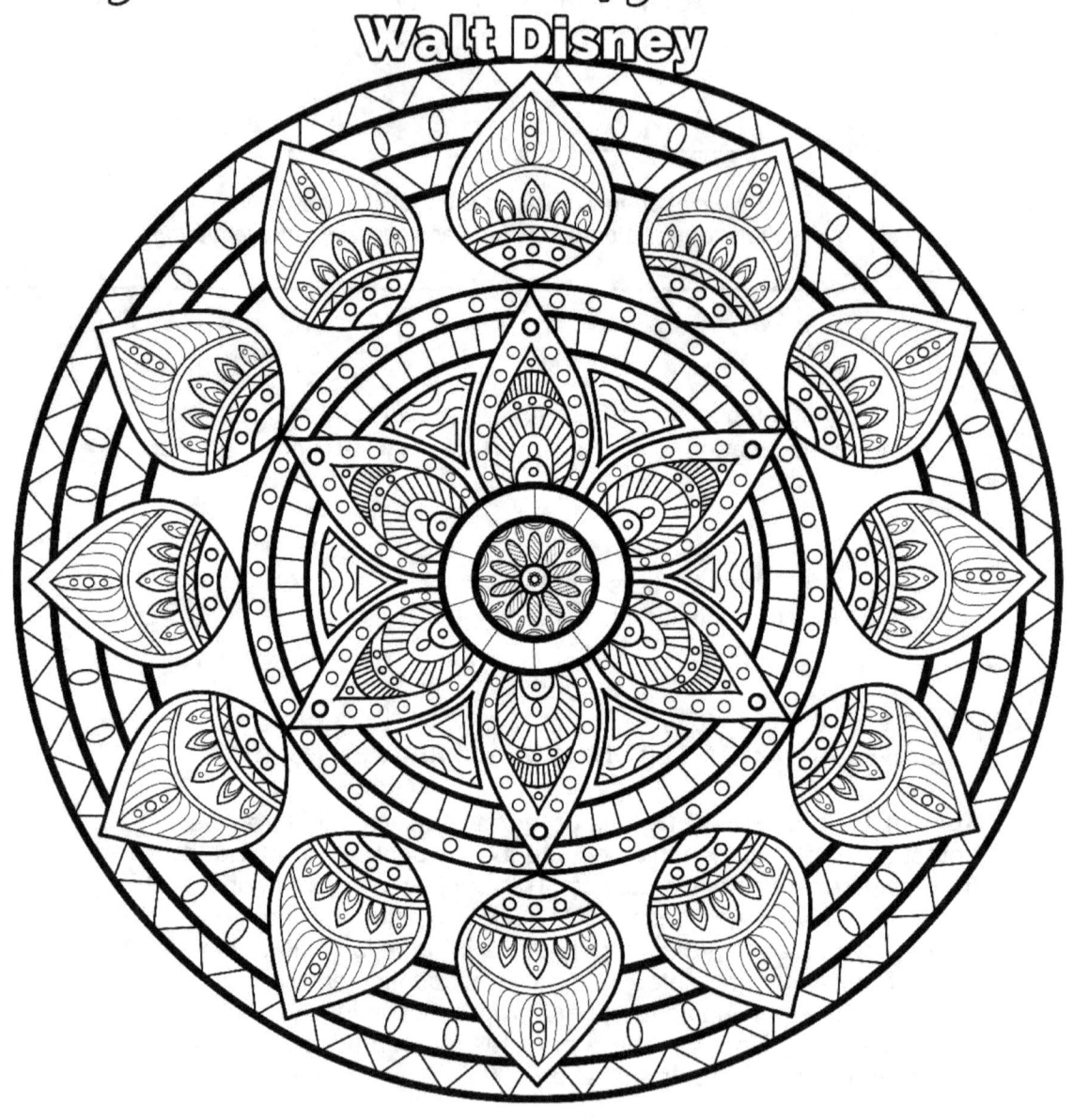

"LIFE IS ABOUT MAKING AN IMPACT, NOT MAKING AN INCOME."
KEVIN KRUSE

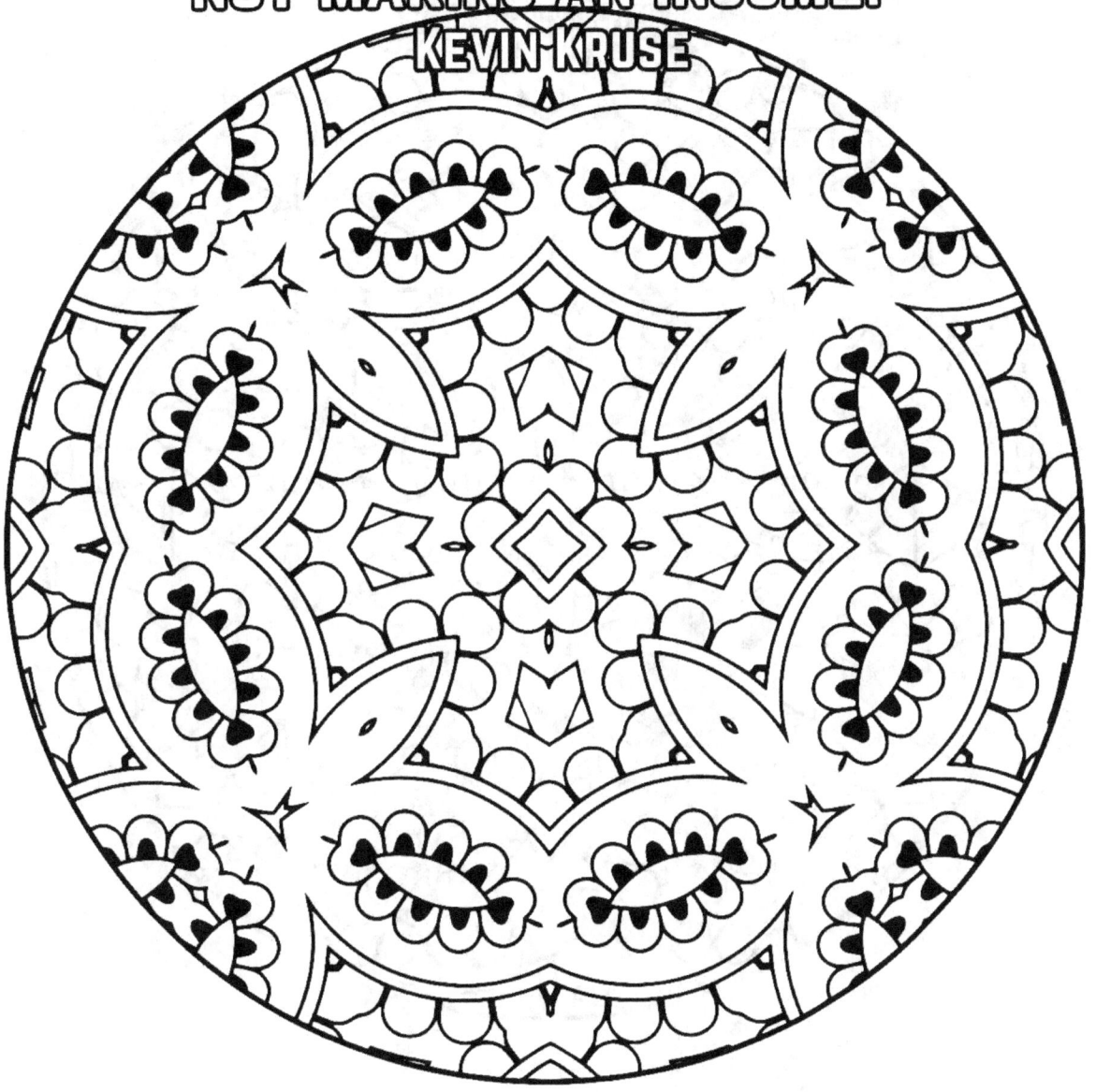

"GO CONFIDENTLY
IN THE DIRECTION OF YOUR DREAMS.
LIVE THE LIFE YOU HAVE IMAGINED."
HENRY DAVID THOREAU

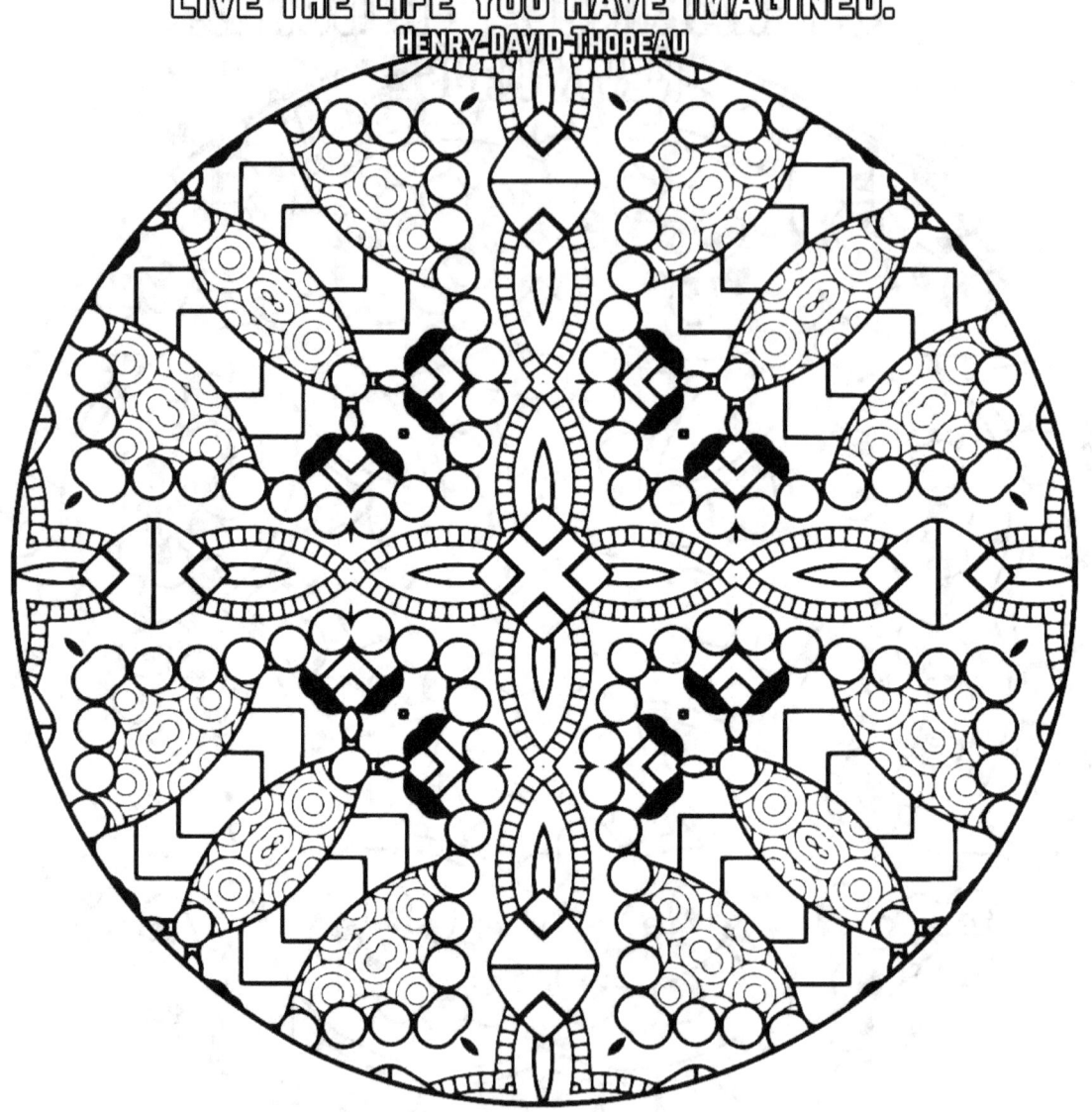

"LEADERSHIP IS DOING WHAT IS RIGHT
WHEN NO ONE IS WATCHING."
George Van Valkenburg

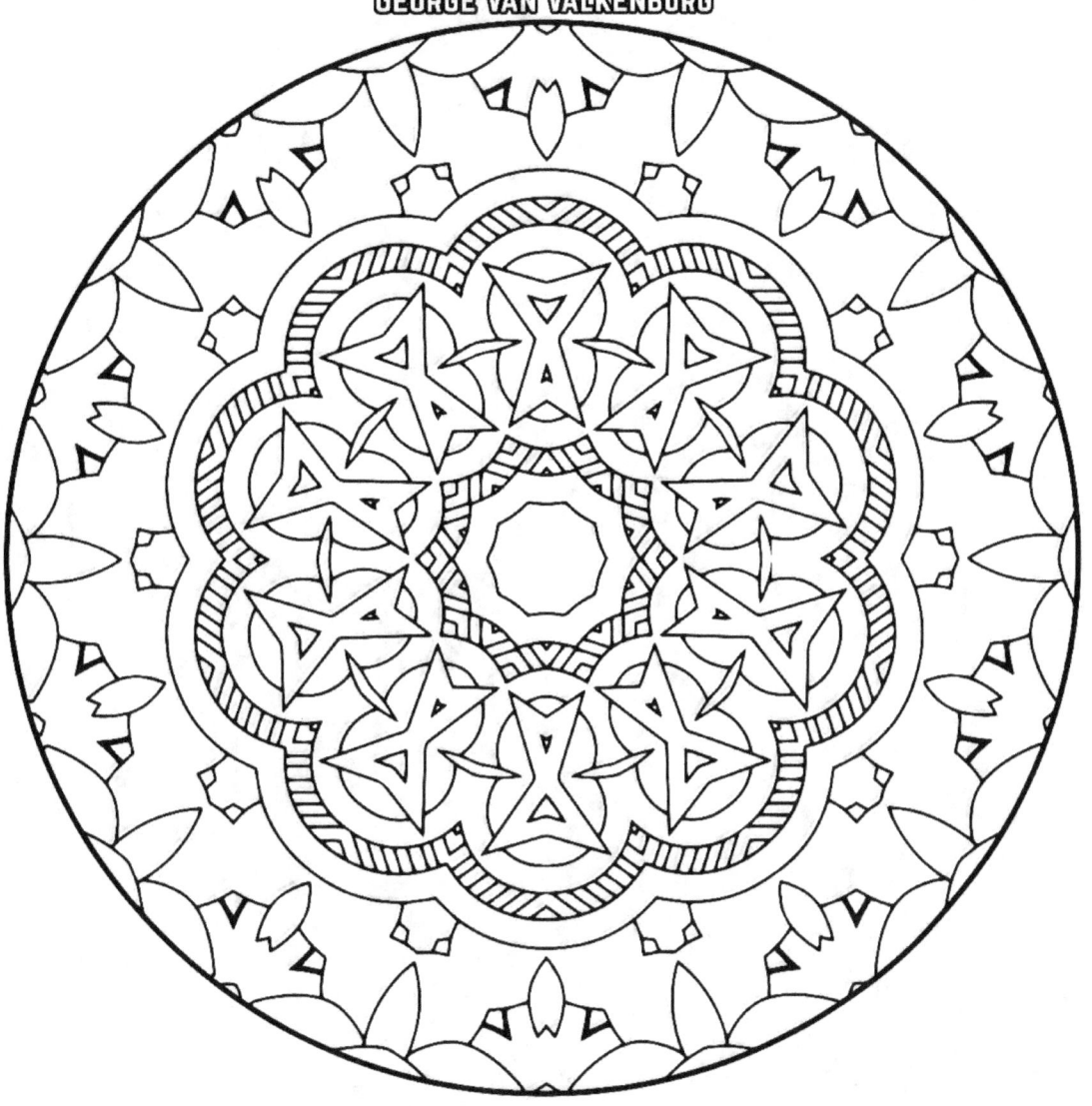

"LEADERSHIP IS DOING WHAT IS RIGHT
WHEN NO ONE IS WATCHING."
GEORGE VAN VALKENBURG

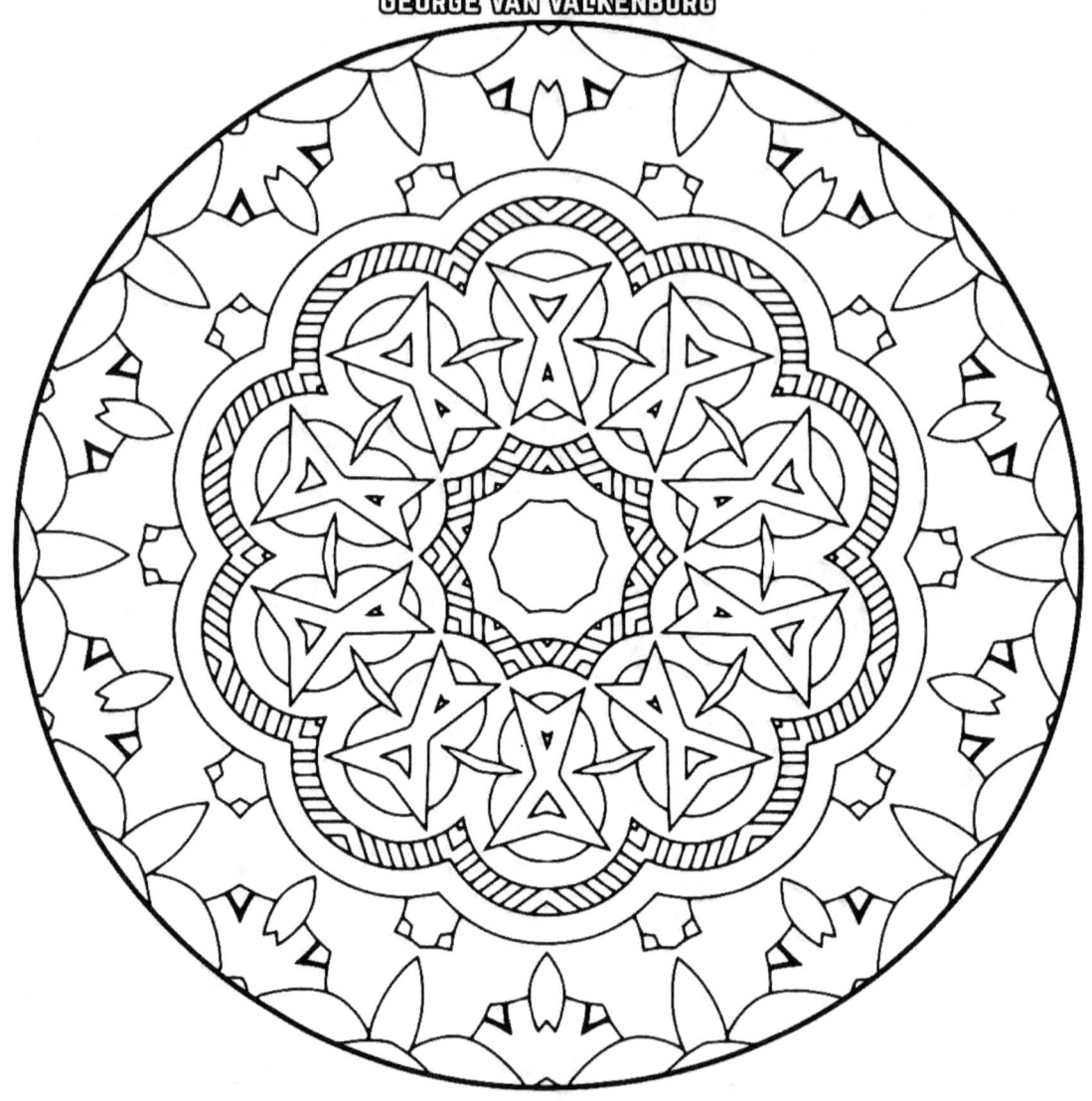

"Go confidently
in the direction of your dreams.
Live the life you have imagined."
Henry David Thoreau

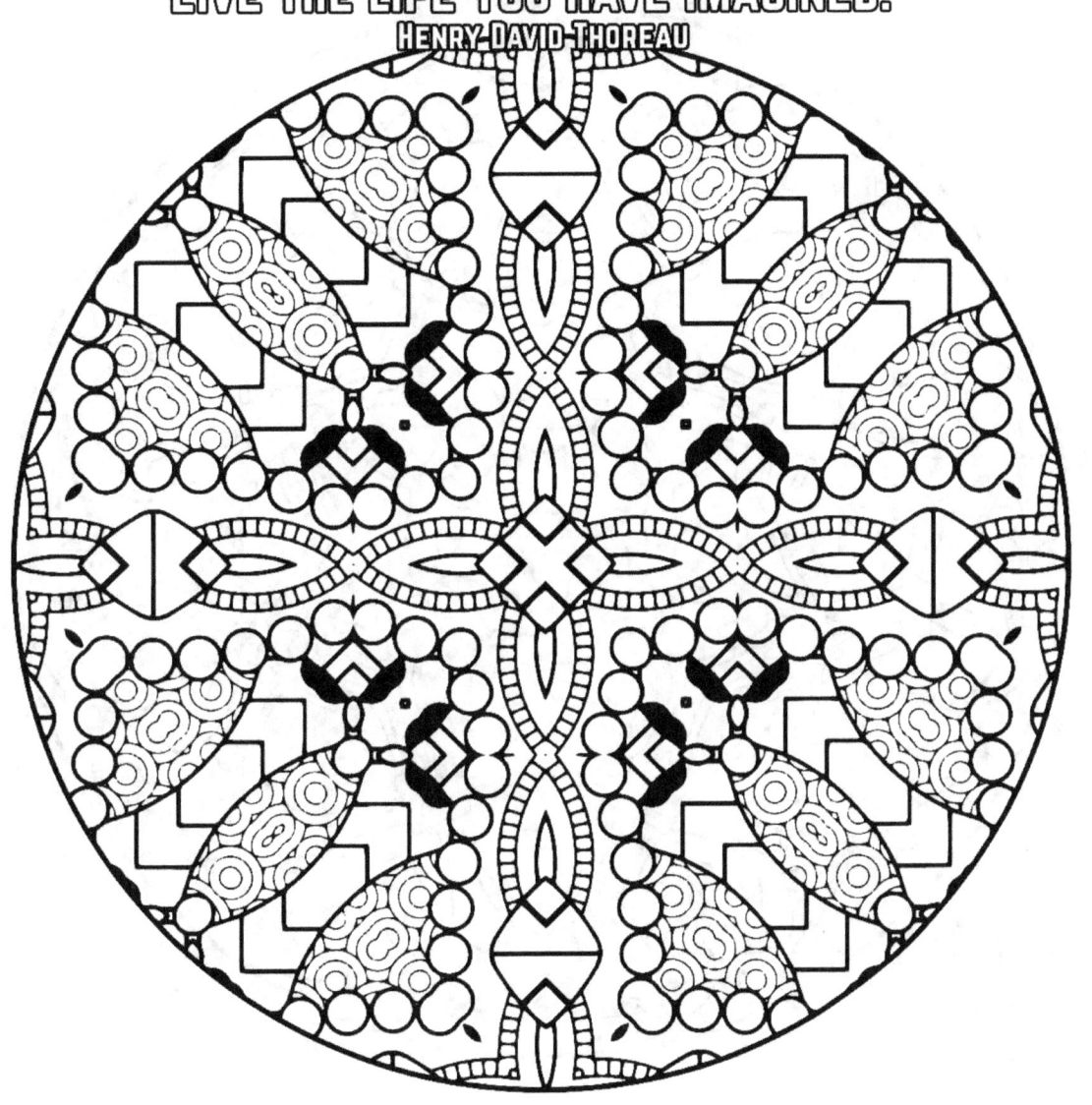

"ALWAYS DO RIGHT;
THIS WILL GRATIFY SOME PEOPLE
AND ASTONISH THE REST."
MARK TWAIN

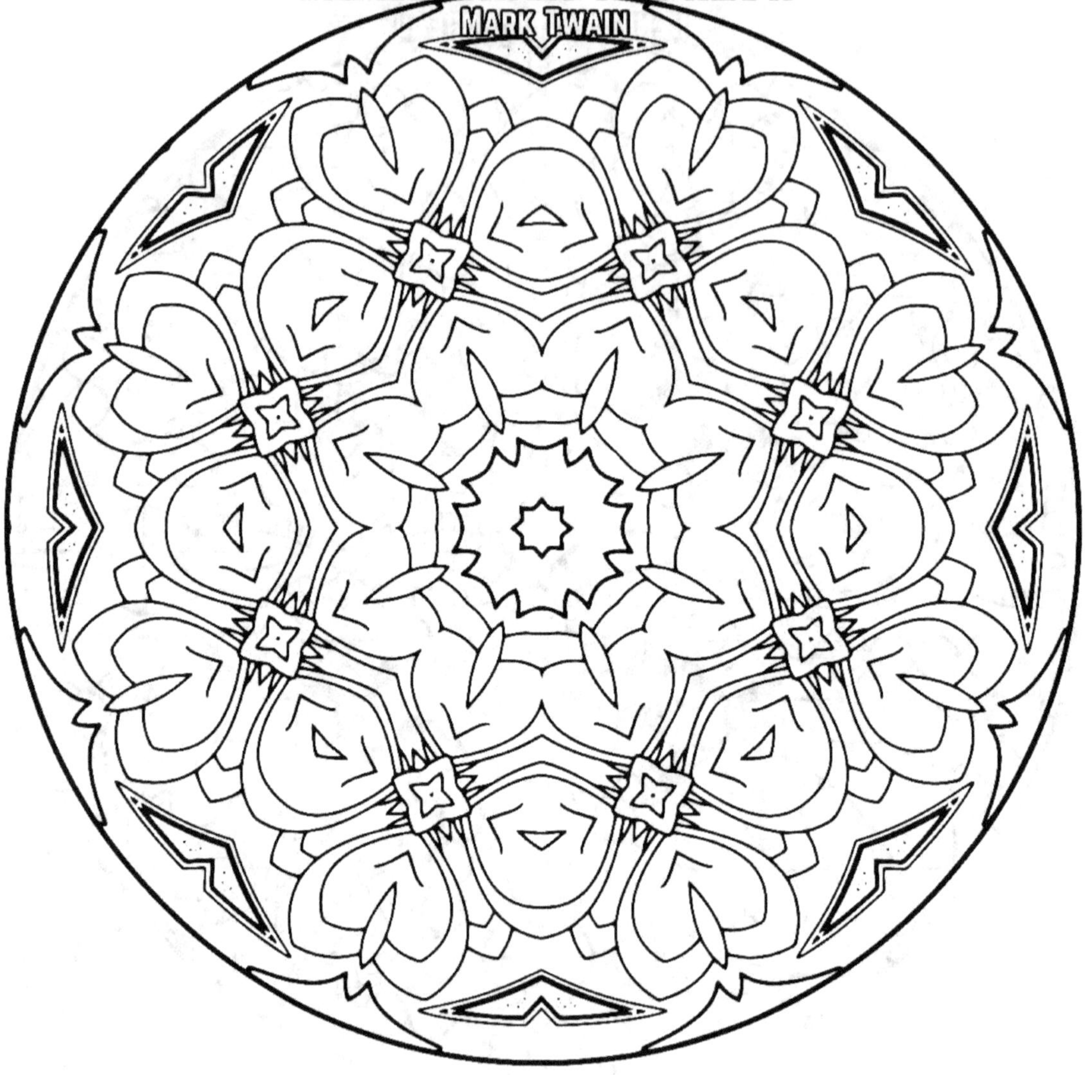

"LIFE IS A BANQUET,
AND MOST POOR SUCKERS ARE STARVING TO DEATH."
ROSALIND RUSSELL

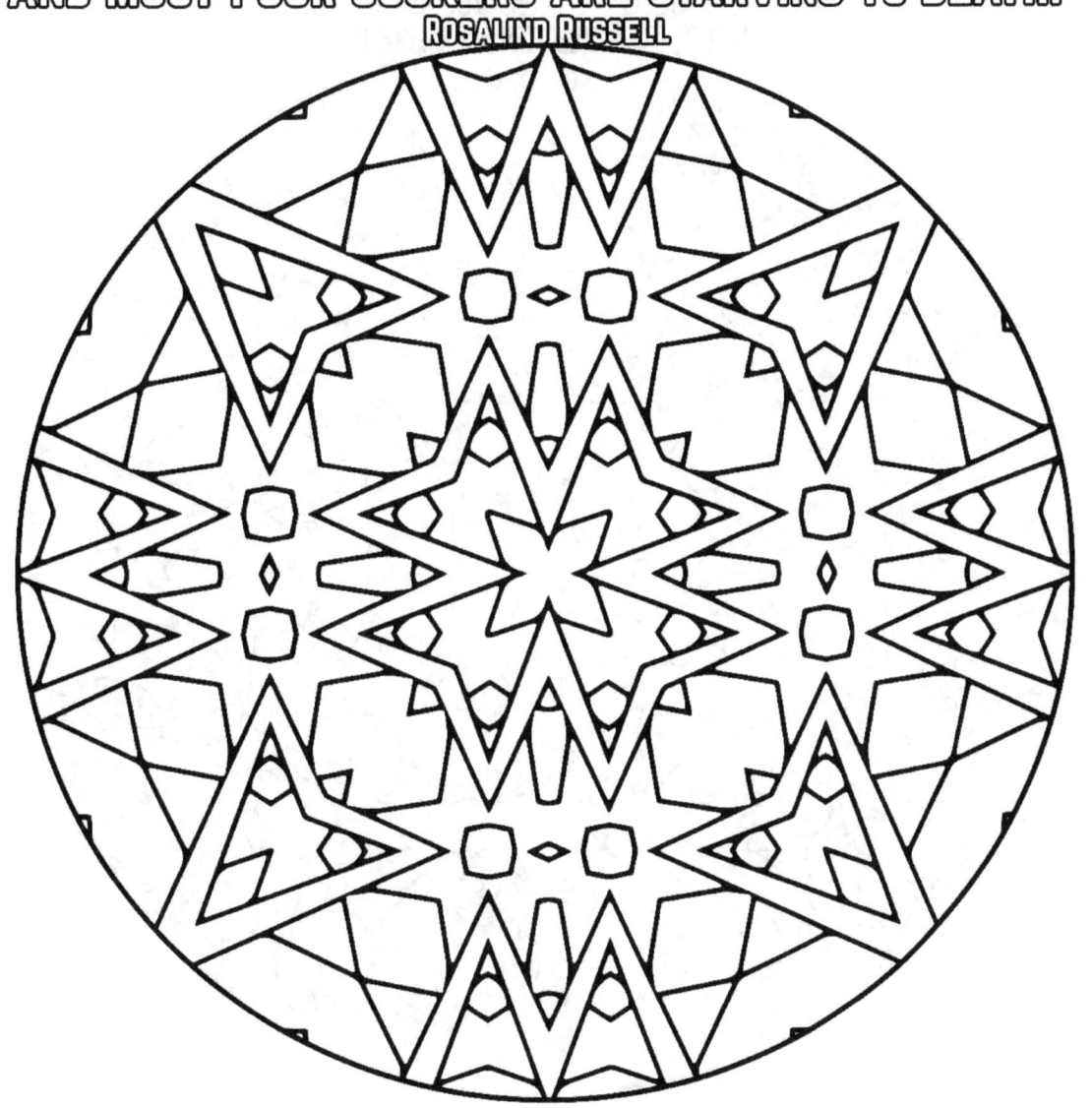

"TO BE PREPARED
IS HALF THE VICTORY."
MIGUEL DE CERVANTES SAAVEDRA

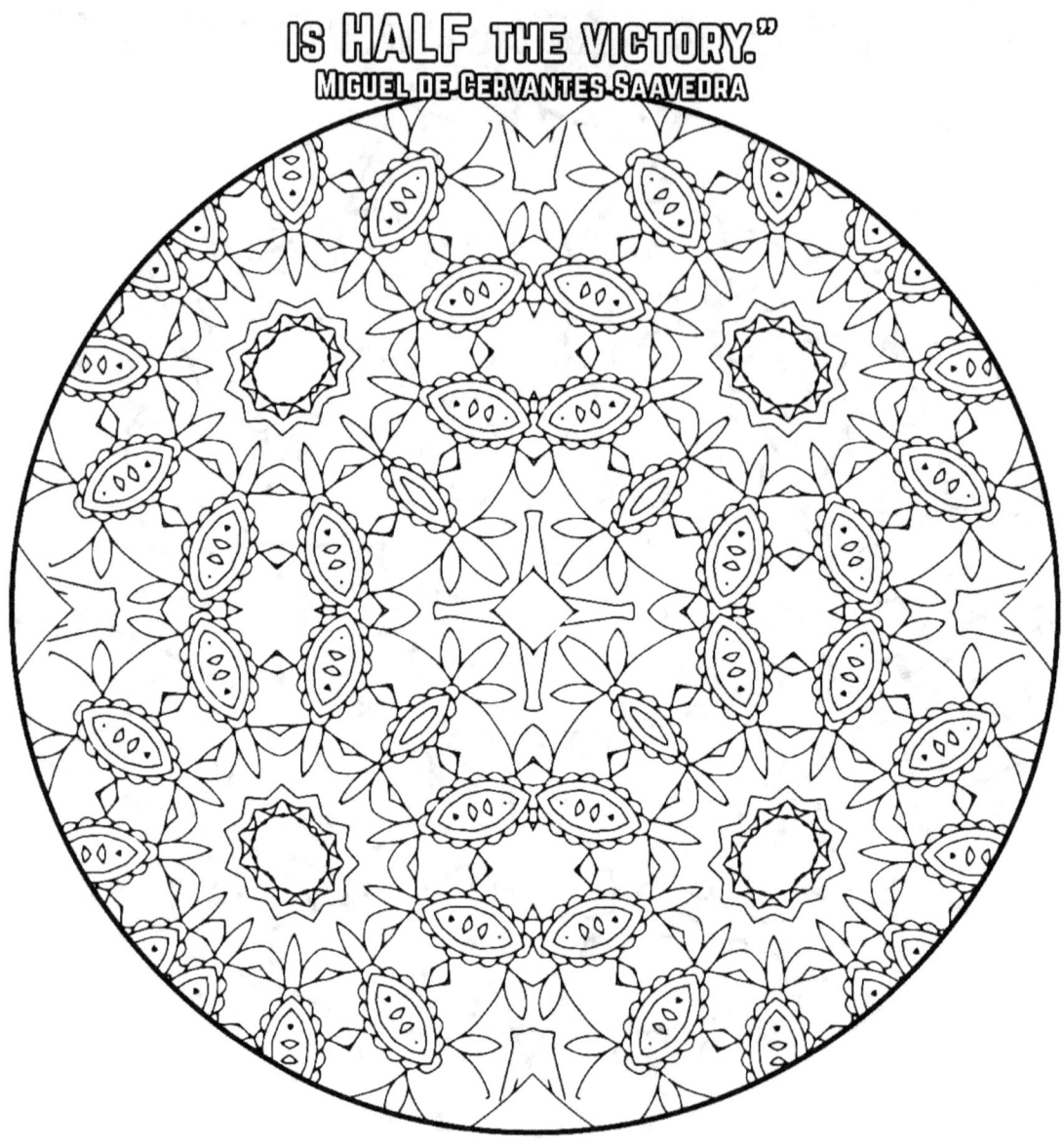

"YOU CAN DISCOVER MORE ABOUT A PERSON
IN AN HOUR OF PLAY
THAN IN A YEAR OF CONVERSATION."
PLATO

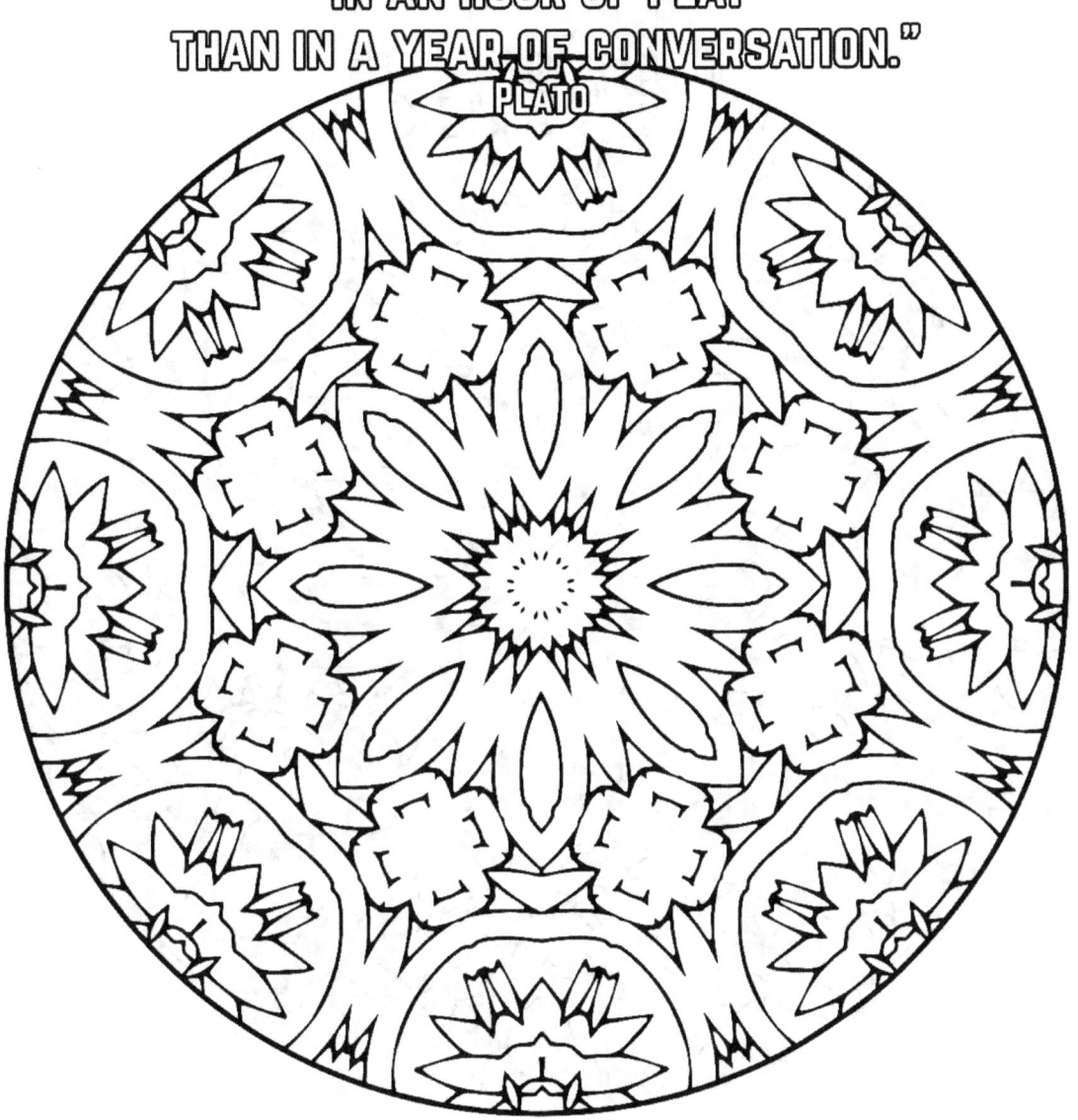

"HE WHO LAUGHS,
LASTS!"
MARY PETTIBONE POOLE

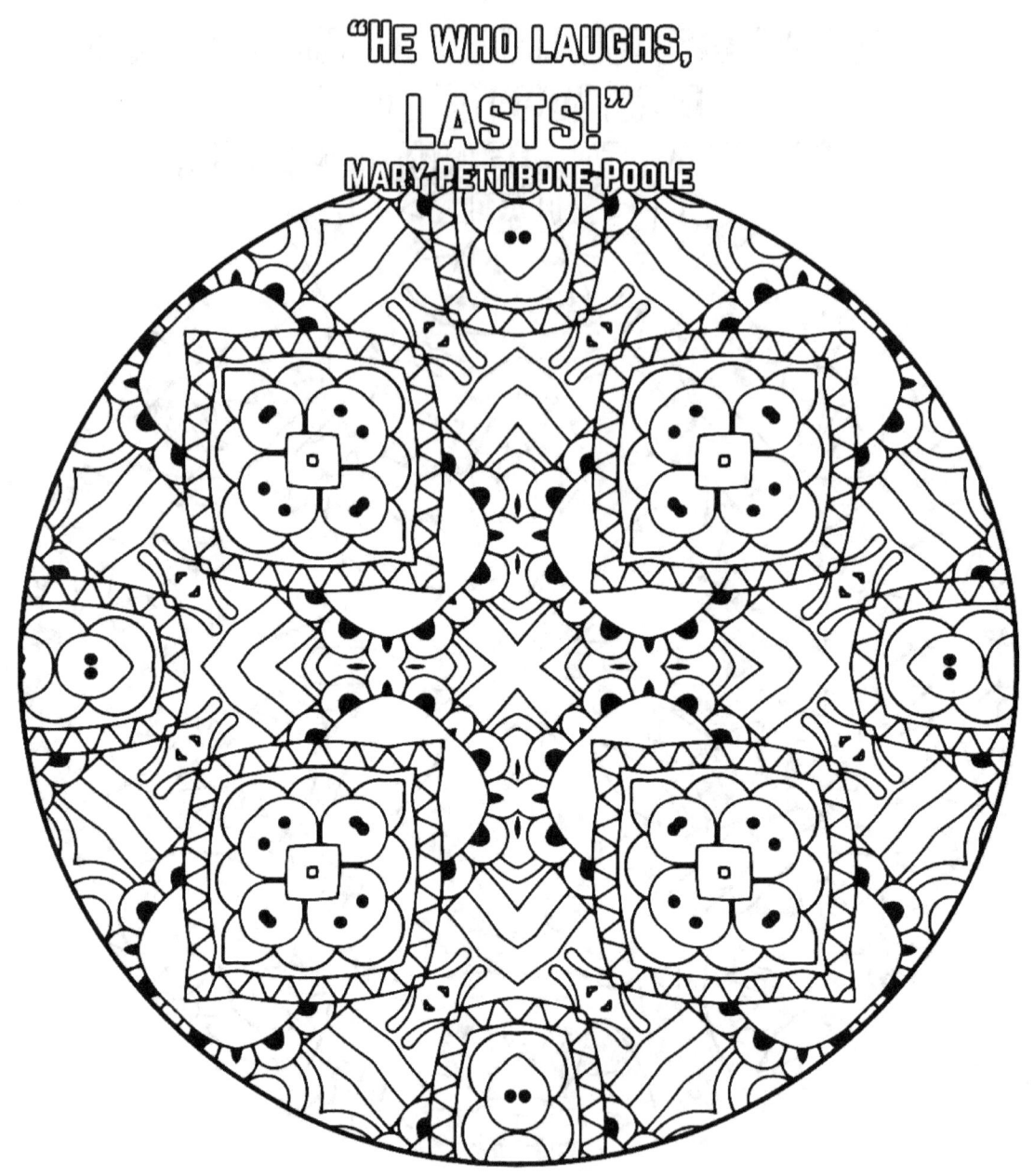

"MAN'S MIND,
ONCE STRETCHED BY A NEW IDEA,
NEVER REGAINS ITS ORIGINAL DIMENSIONS."
OLIVER WENDELL HOLMES

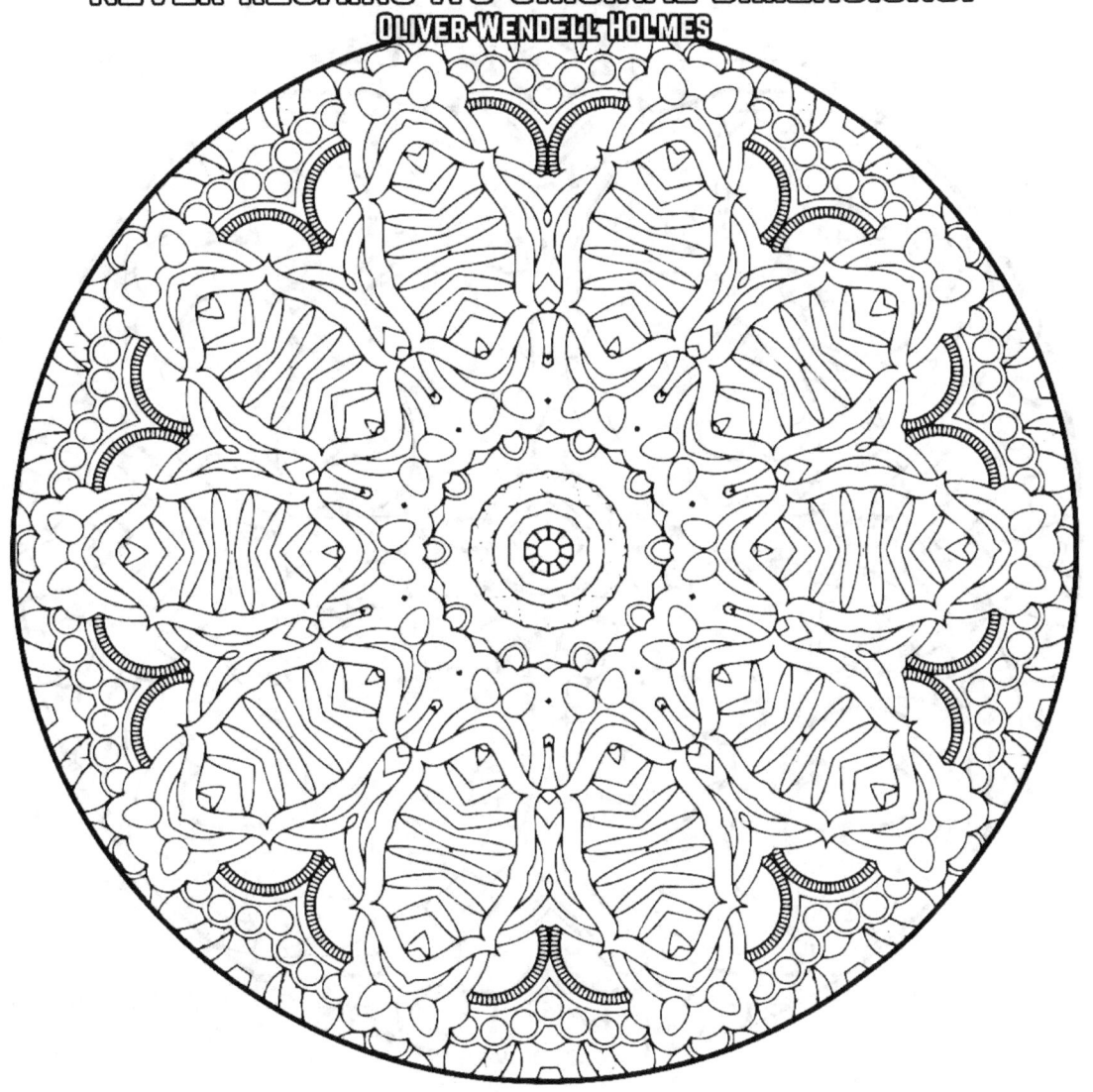

"JUDGE A TREE FROM ITS FRUIT,
NOT FROM ITS LEAVES."
EURIPIDES

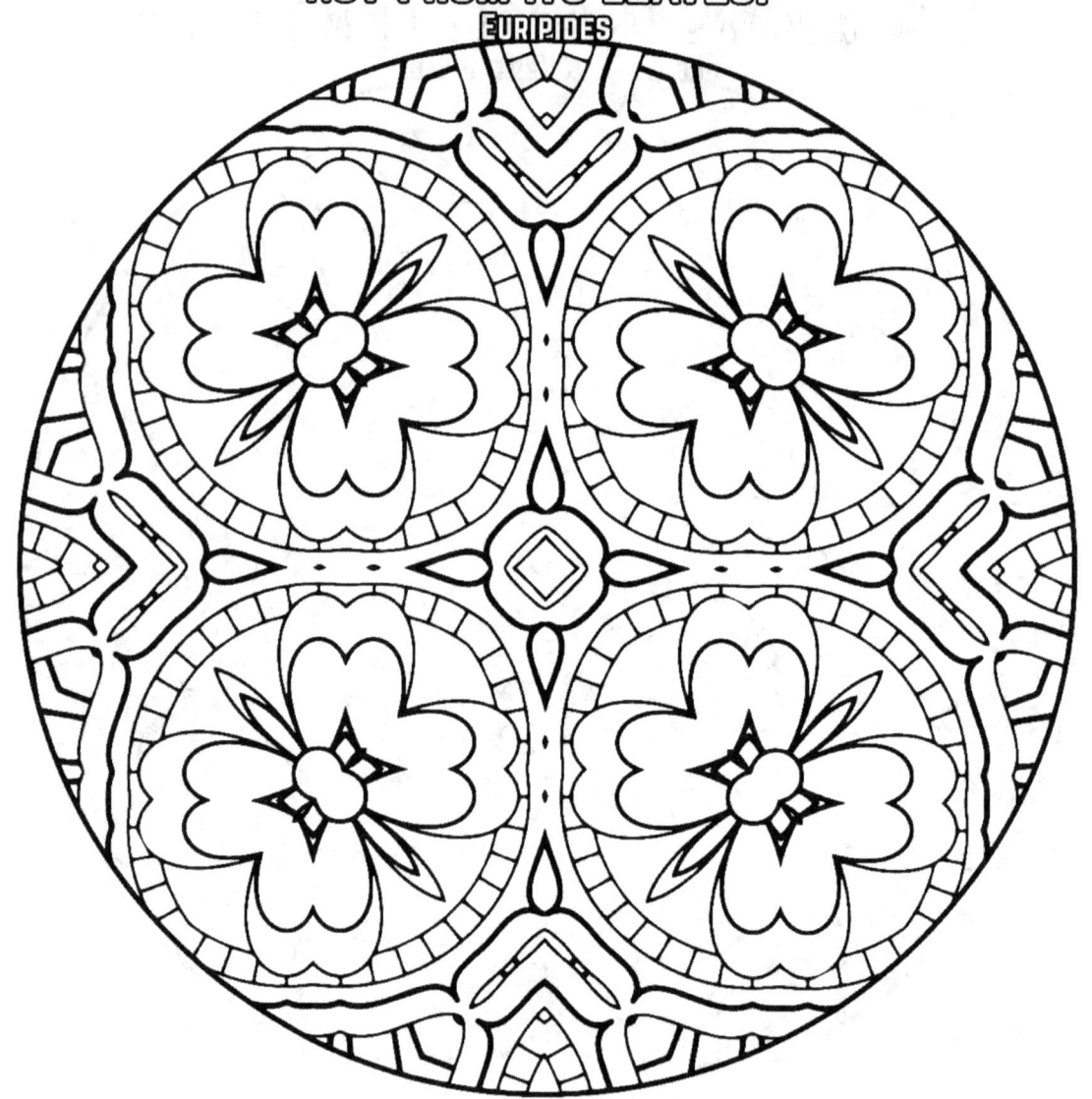

"FOR EVERY MINUTE YOU REMAIN ANGRY,
YOU GIVE UP 60 SECONDS OF PEACE OF MIND."
F. SCOTT FITZGERALD

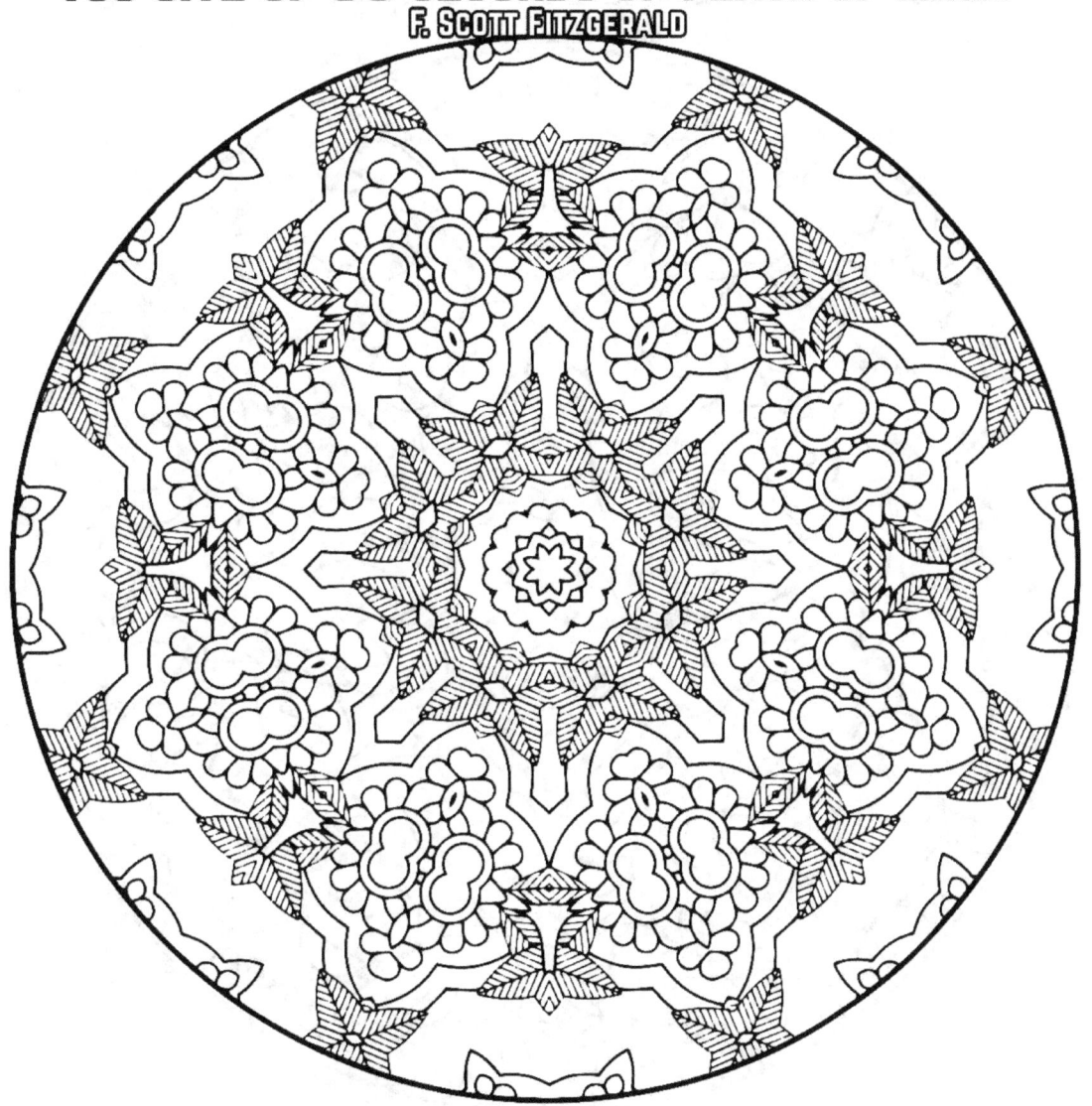

"A BIRD DOESN'T SING BECAUSE IT HAS AN ANSWER;
IT SINGS BECAUSE IT HAS A SONG."
MAYA ANGELOU

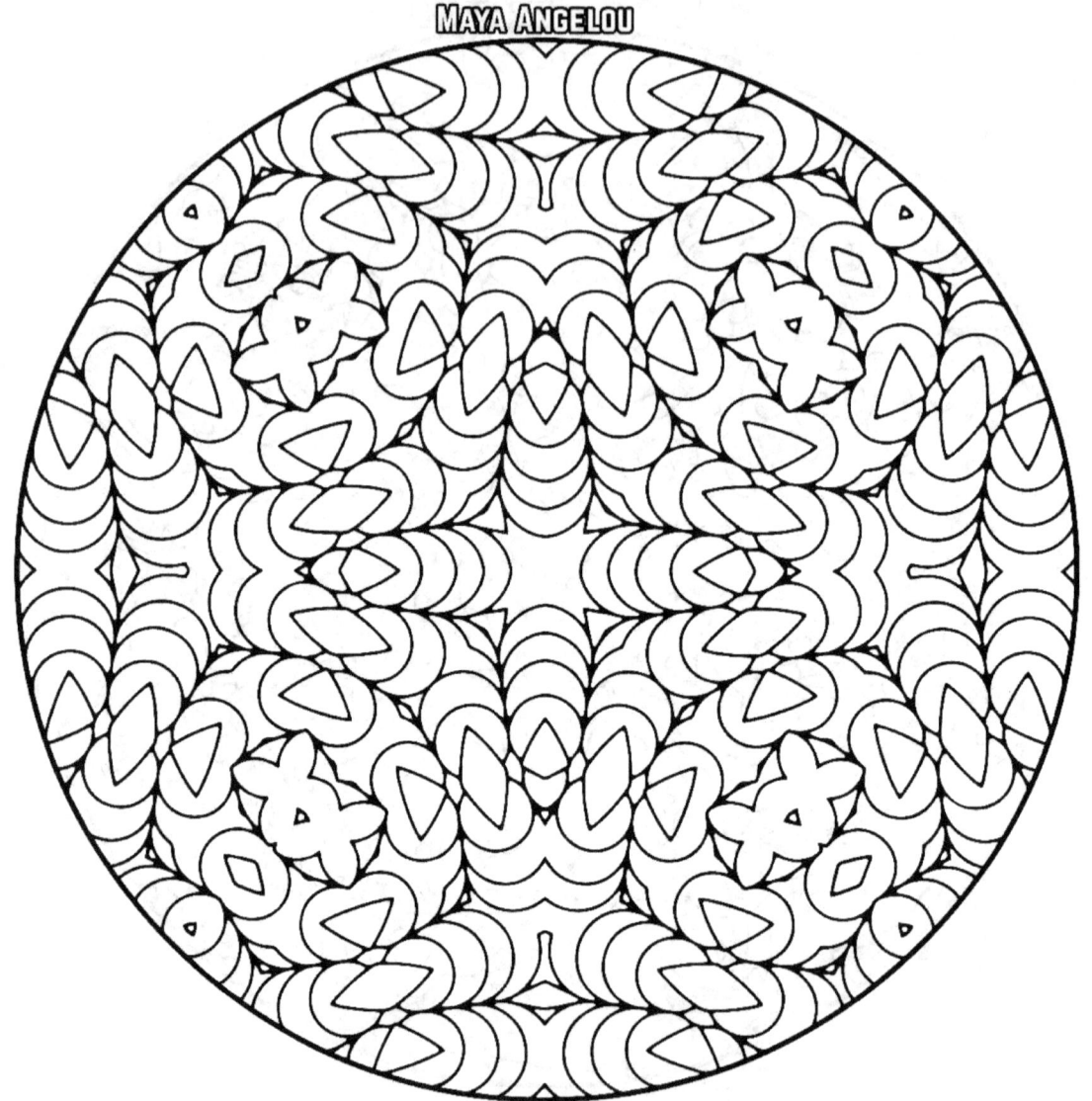

"WE ARE WHAT WE REPEATEDLY DO.
EXCELLENCE, THEN, IS NOT AN ACT,
BUT A HABIT."
ARISTOTLE

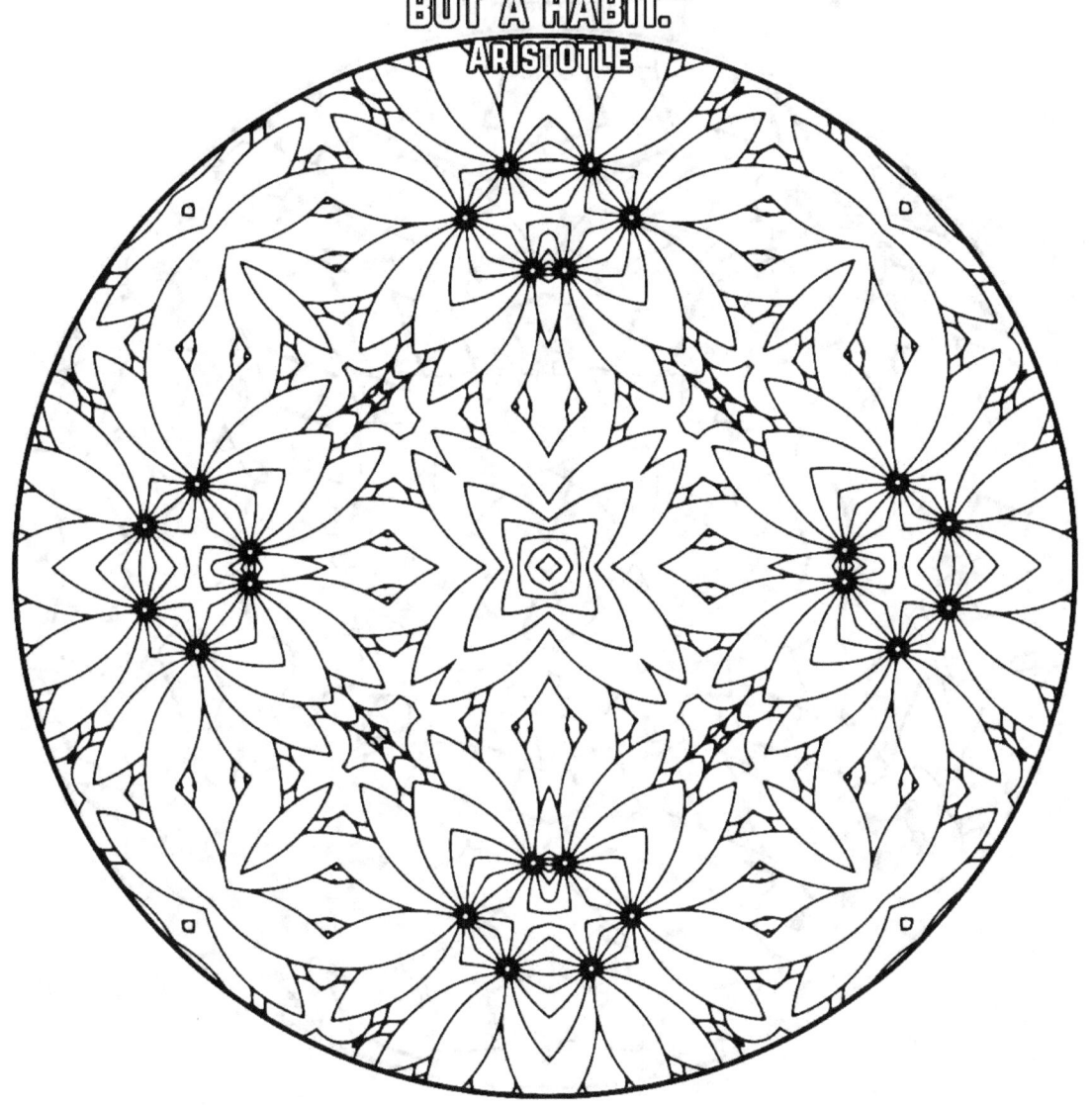

"A BAD ATTITUDE IS LIKE A FLAT TIRE,
YOU CAN'T GO ANYWHERE UNTIL YOU CHANGE IT."
Unknown

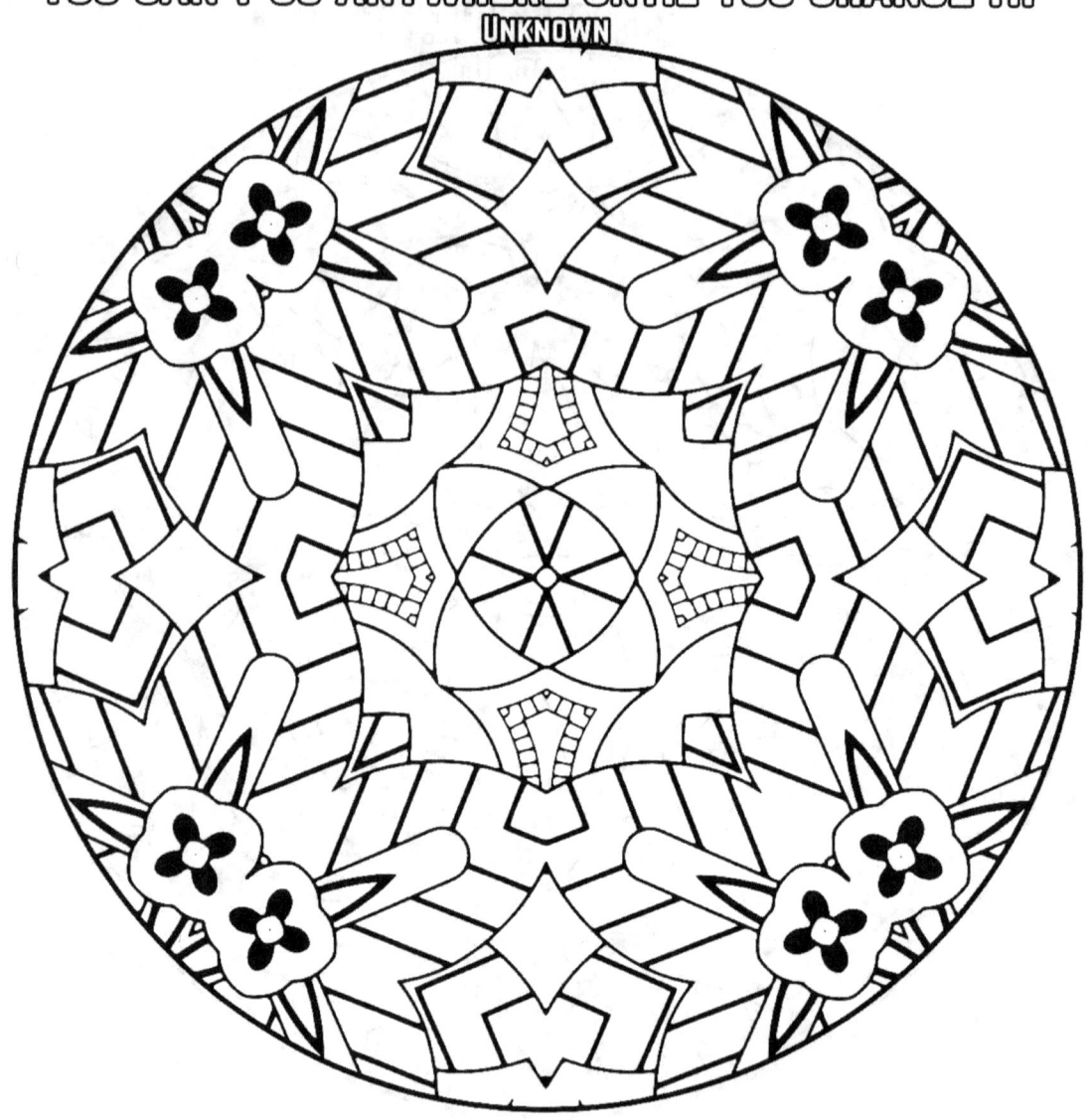

"DON'T LET YESTERDAY
USE UP TOO MUCH OF TODAY."
CHEROKEE PROVERB

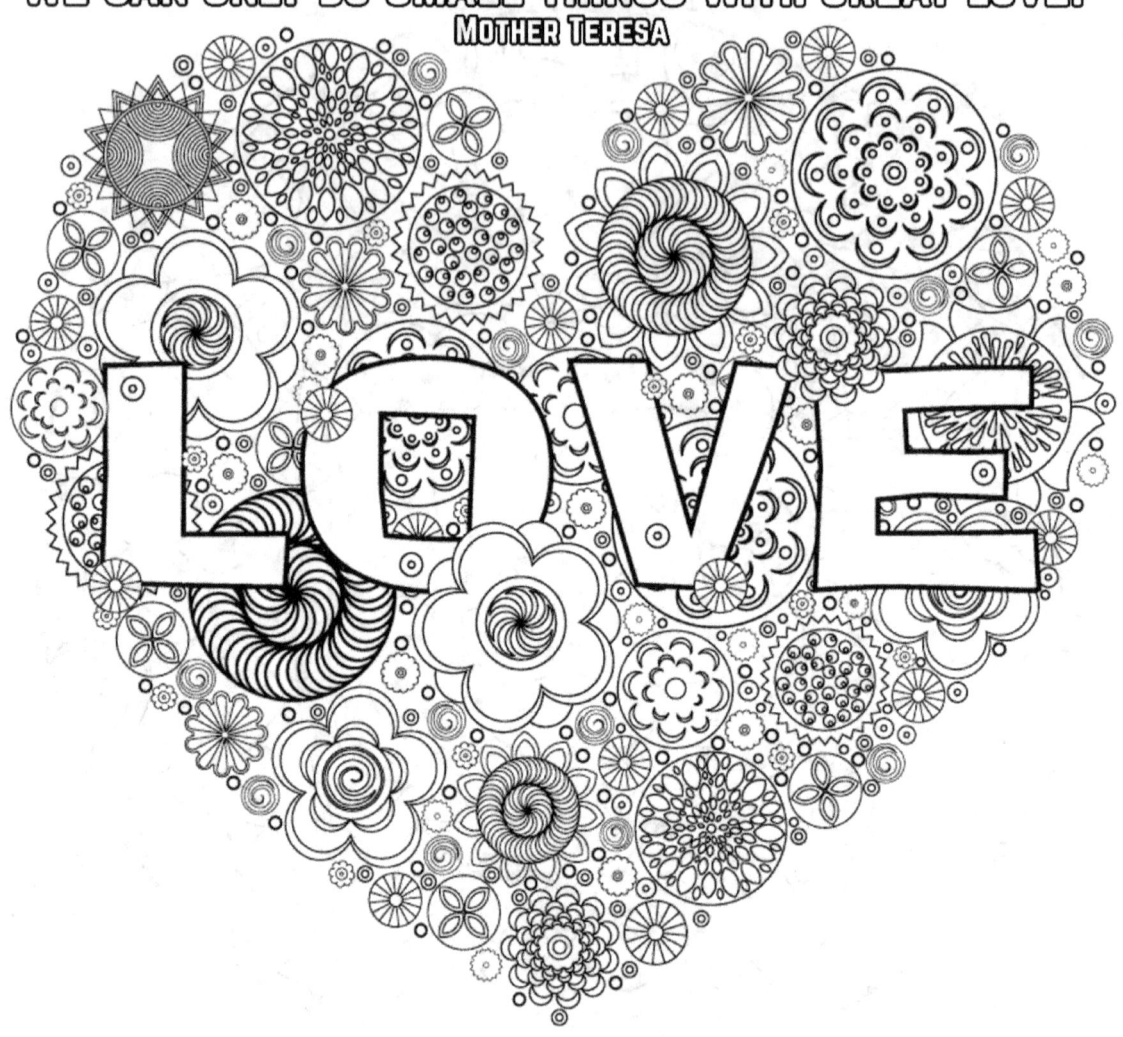

"IN THIS LIFE WE CANNOT DO GREAT THINGS.
WE CAN ONLY DO SMALL THINGS WITH GREAT LOVE."
MOTHER TERESA

"I KNOW THE PRICE OF SUCCESS:
DEDICATION, HARD WORK,
AND AN UNREMITTING DEVOTION
TO THE THINGS YOU WANT TO SEE HAPPEN."
FRANK LLOYD WRIGHT

"OBSTACLES ARE THOSE FRIGHTFUL THINGS YOU SEE
WHEN YOU TAKE YOUR EYES OFF YOUR GOAL."
HENRY FORD

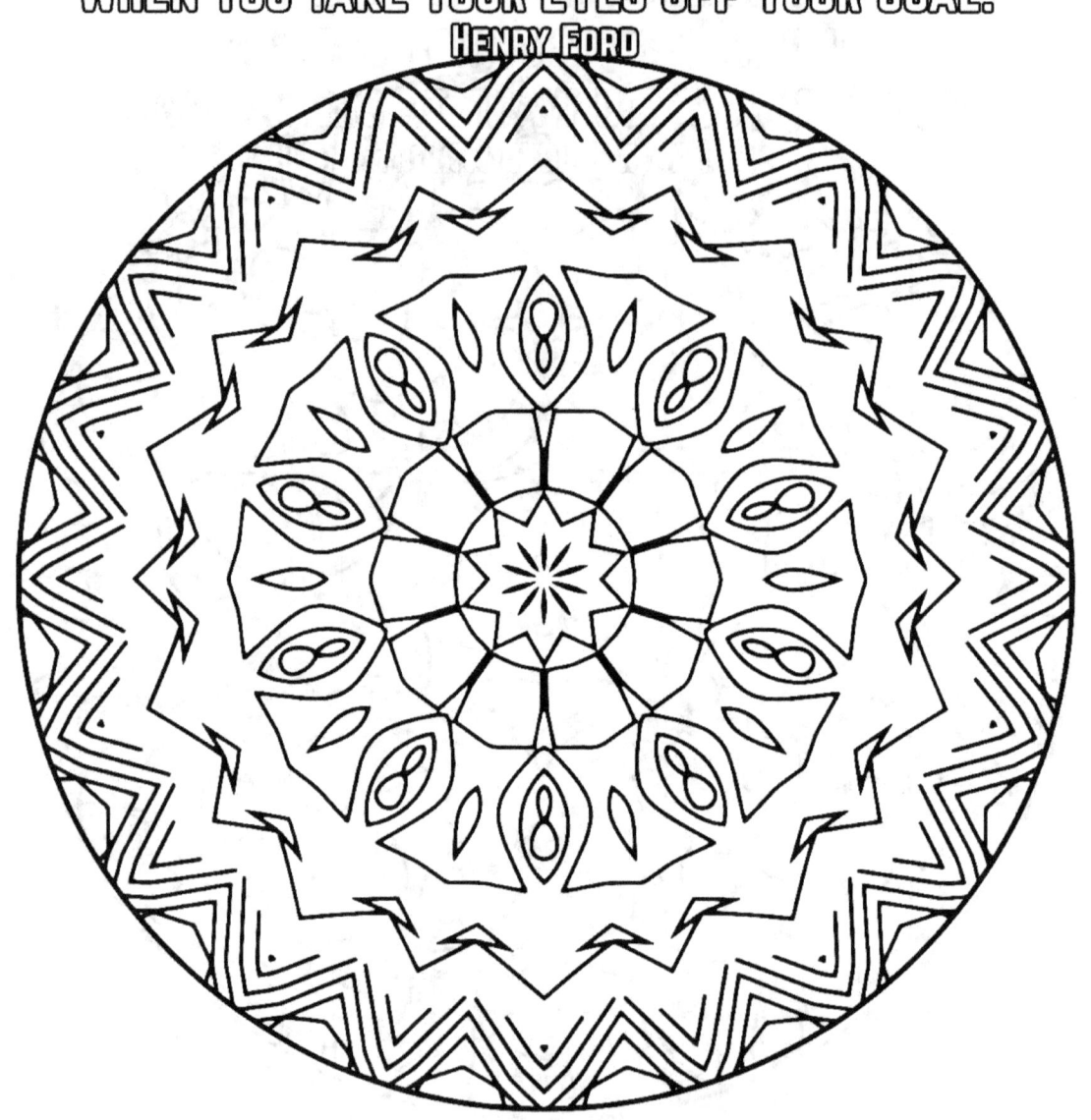

"TO ACCOMPLISH GREAT THINGS,
WE MUST NOT ONLY ACT,
BUT ALSO DREAM;
NOT ONLY PLAN, BUT ALSO BELIEVE."
ANATOLE FRANCE

"THE JOURNEY IS THE REWARD."
CHINESE PROVERB

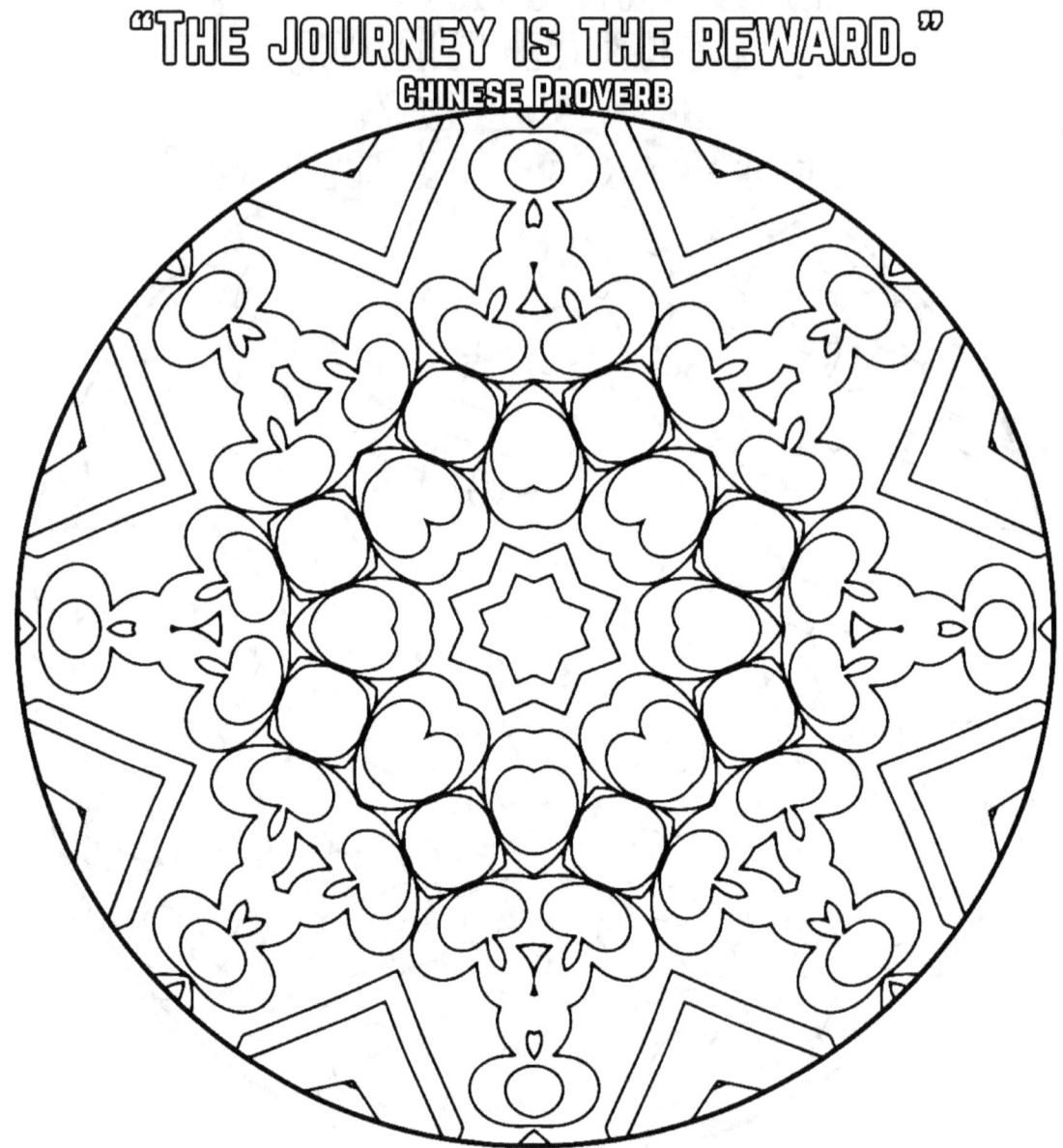

"KITES RISE HIGHEST AGAINST THE WIND;
NOT WITH IT."
WINSTON CHURCHILL

"HOPE IS A WAKING DREAM."
ARISTOTLE

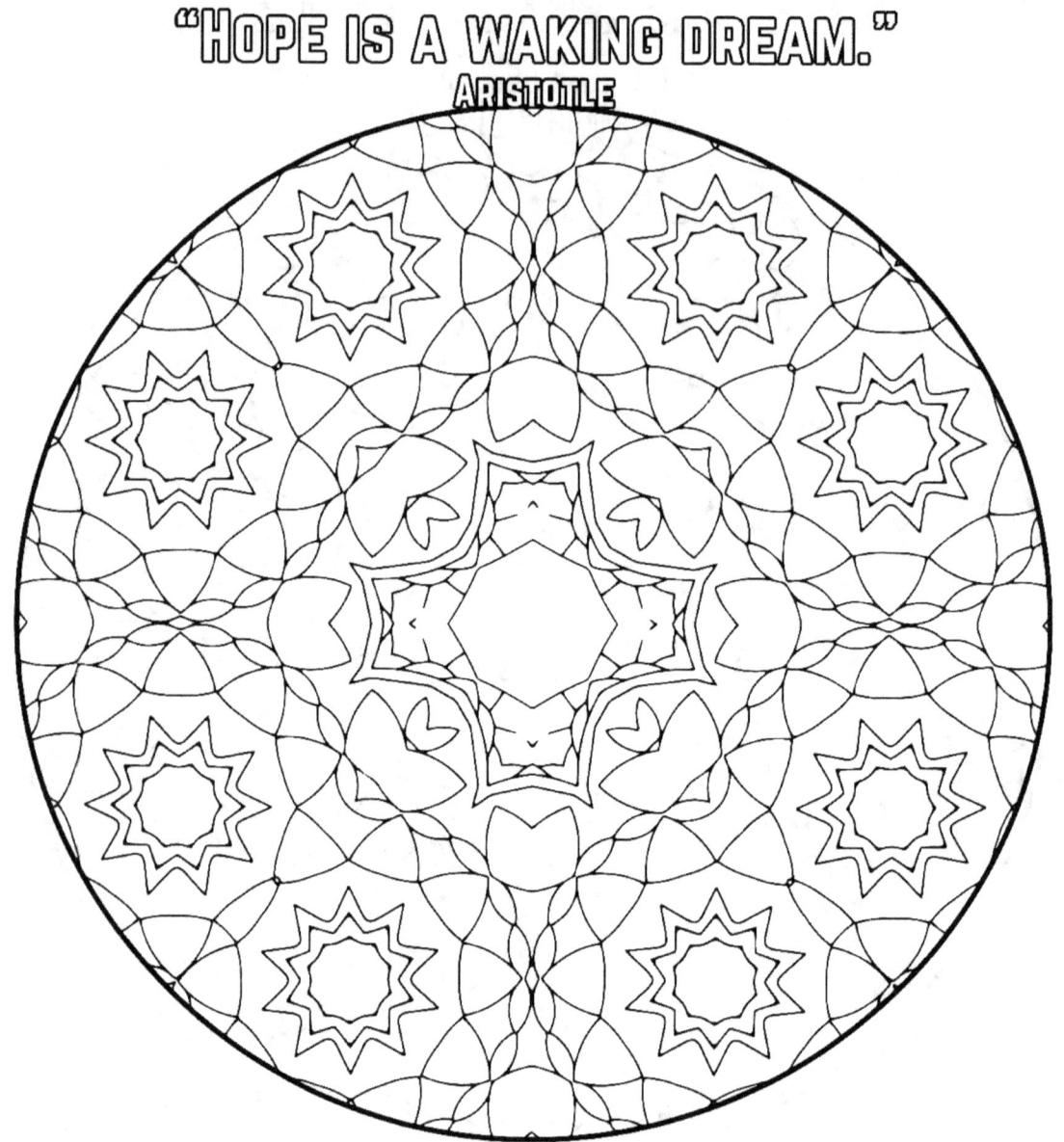

"ONE DAY, YOU'LL BE JUST A MEMORY
FOR SOME PEOPLE.
DO YOUR BEST TO BE A GOOD ONE."
UNKNOWN

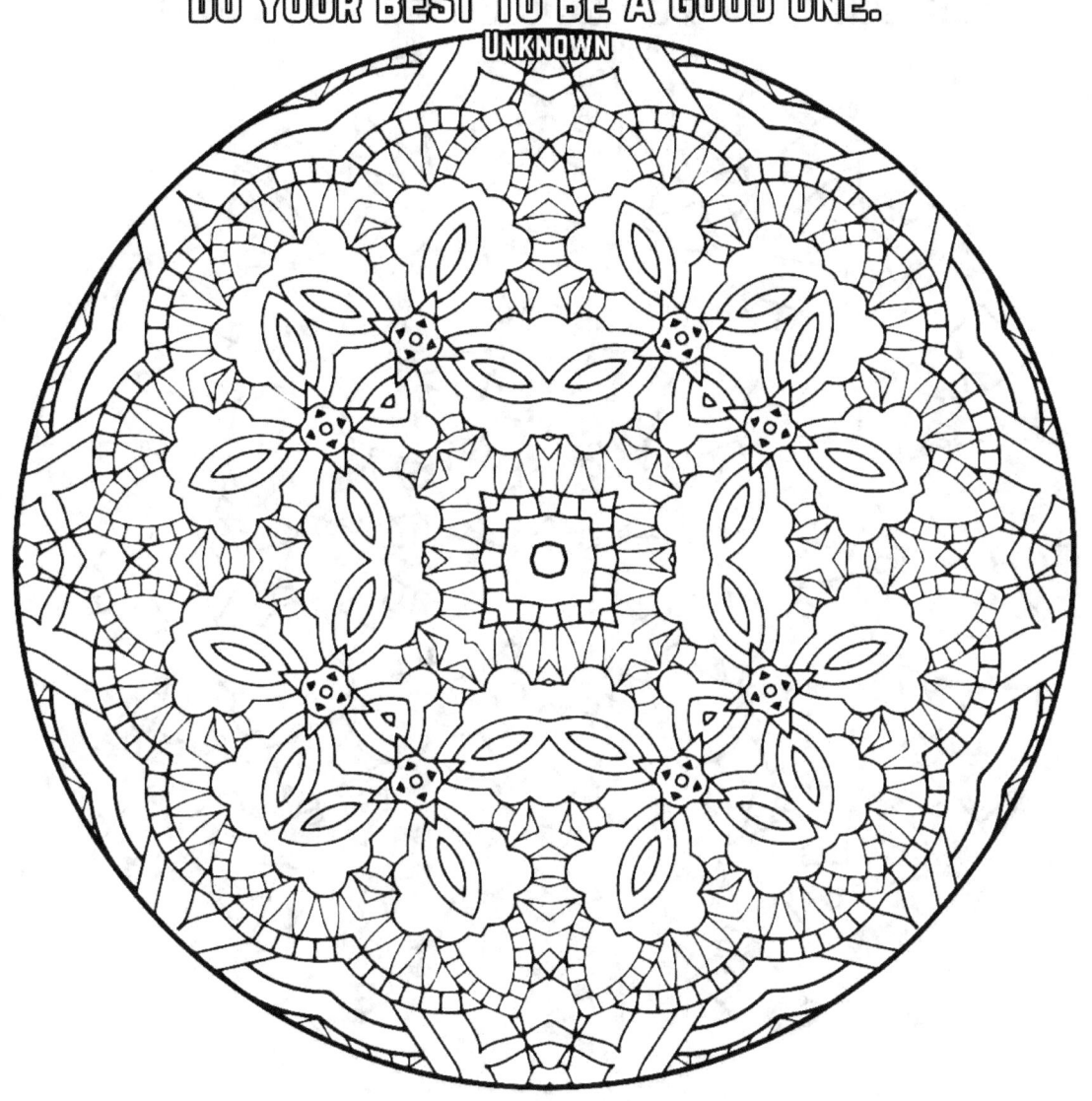

"THE MORE SAND THAT HAS ESCAPED
FROM THE HOURGLASS OF OUR LIFE,
THE CLEARER WE SHOULD SEE THROUGH IT."
NICCOLO MACHIAVELLI

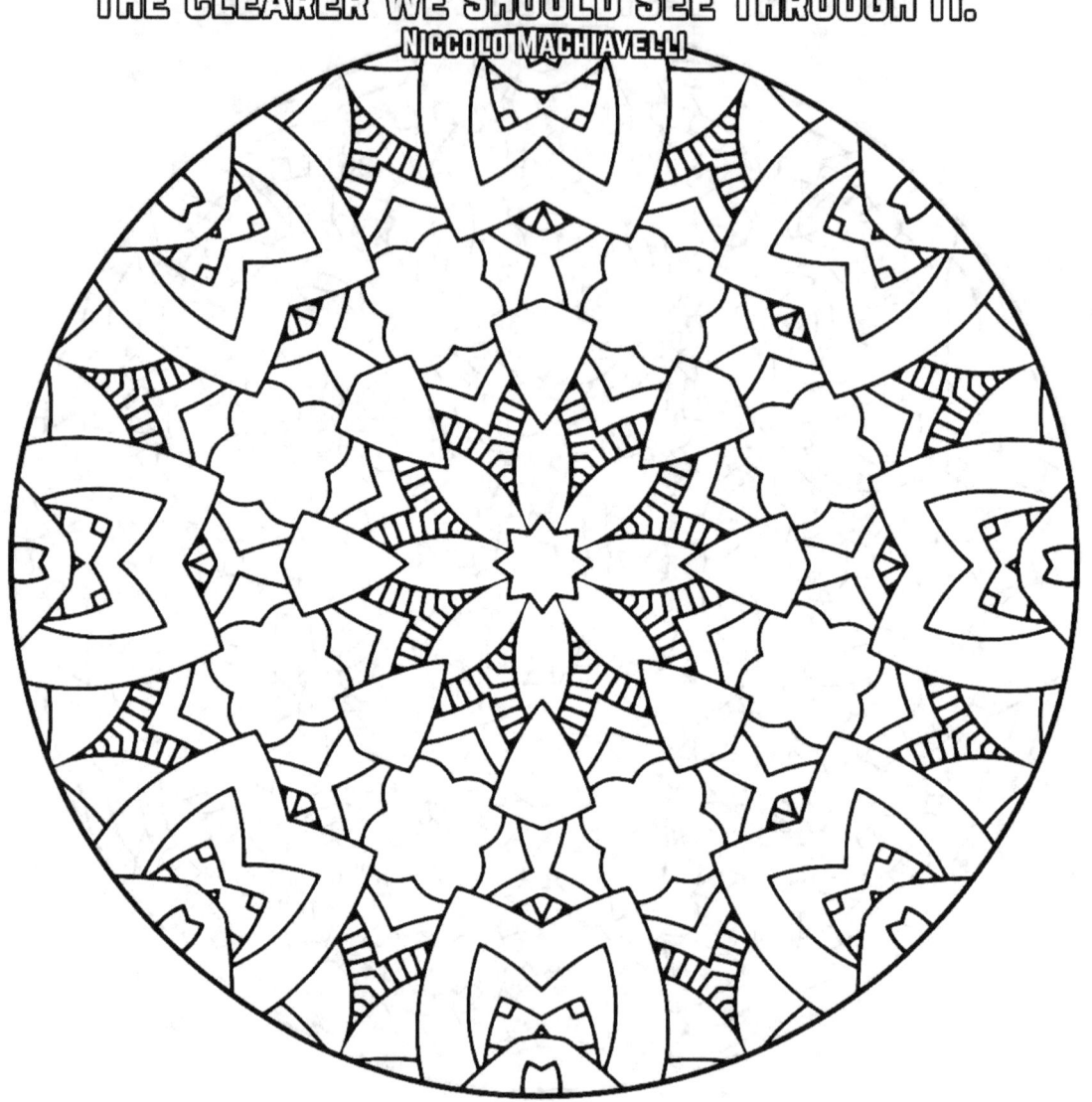

"I KNEW IT COULD BE DONE,
IT HAD TO BE DONE AND I DID IT."
GERTRUDE EDERLE

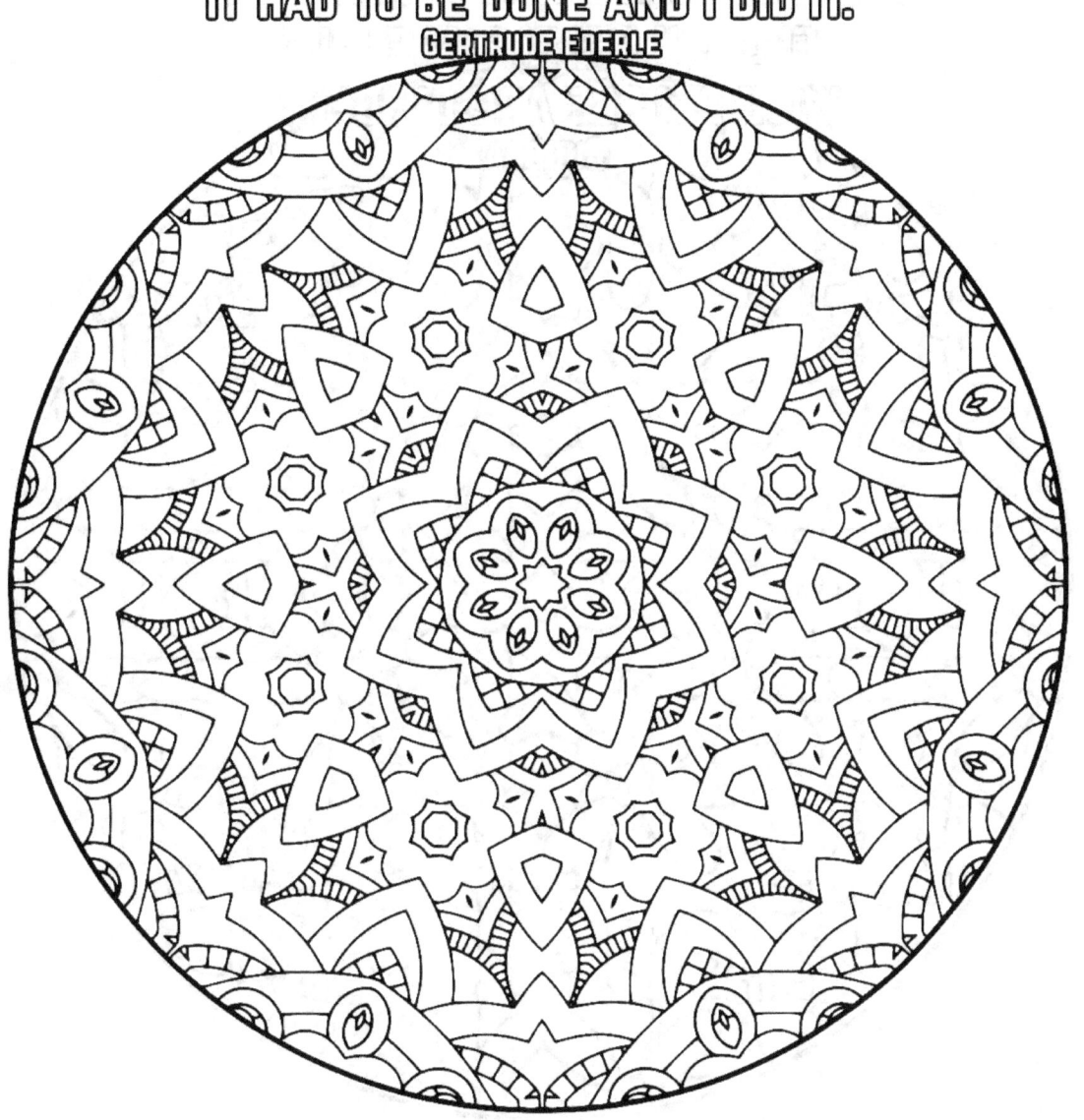

"TO BE IDLE IS A SHORT ROAD TO DEATH
AND TO BE DILIGENT IS A WAY OF LIFE;
FOOLISH PEOPLE ARE IDLE,
WISE PEOPLE ARE DILIGENT."
BUDDHA

"SOMEONE'S SITTING IN THE SHADE TODAY
BECAUSE
SOMEONE PLANTED A TREE A LONG TIME AGO."
WARREN BUFFETT

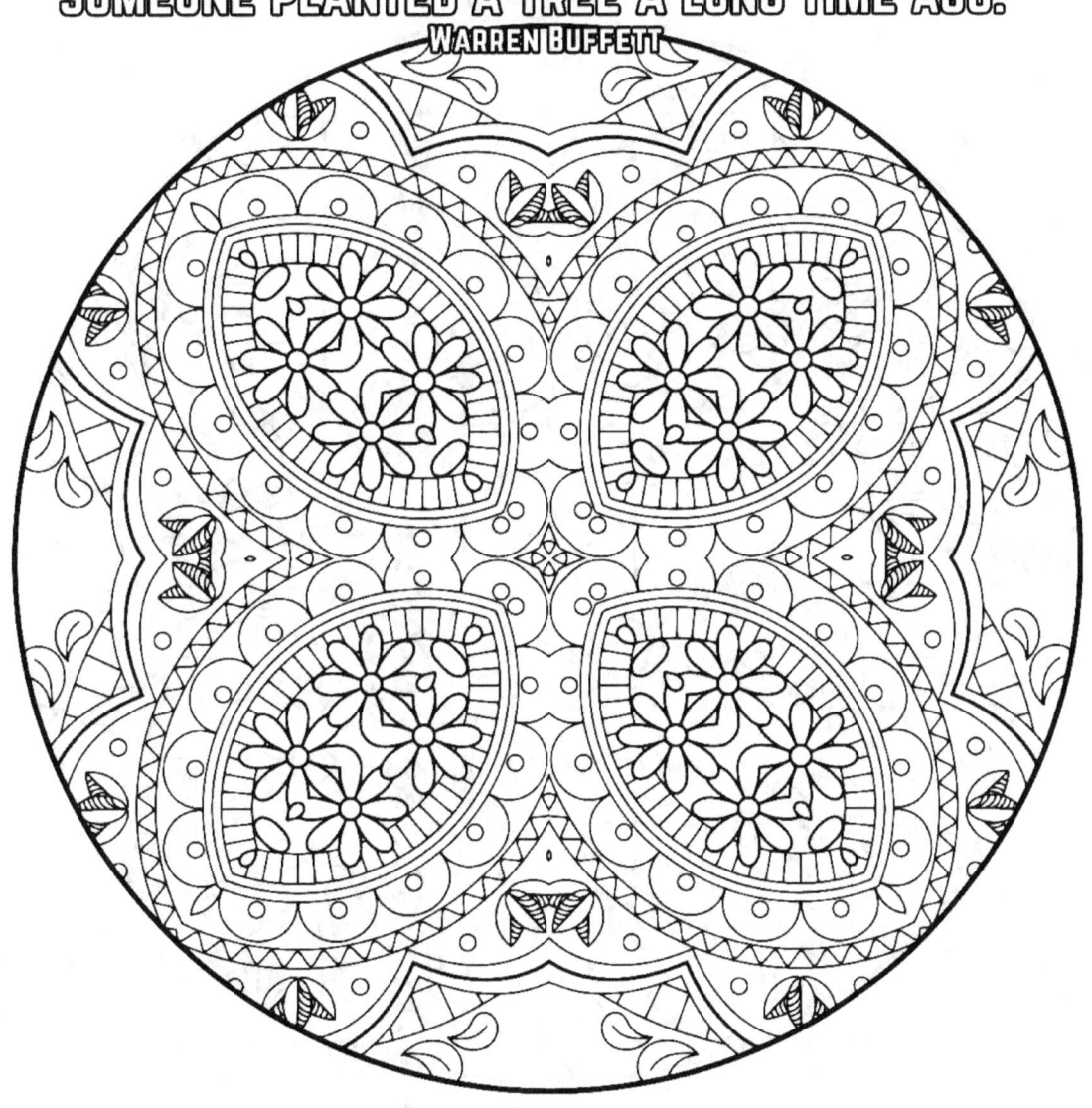

"ARRIVING AT ONE POINT
IS THE STARTING POINT TO ANOTHER."
JOHN DEWEY

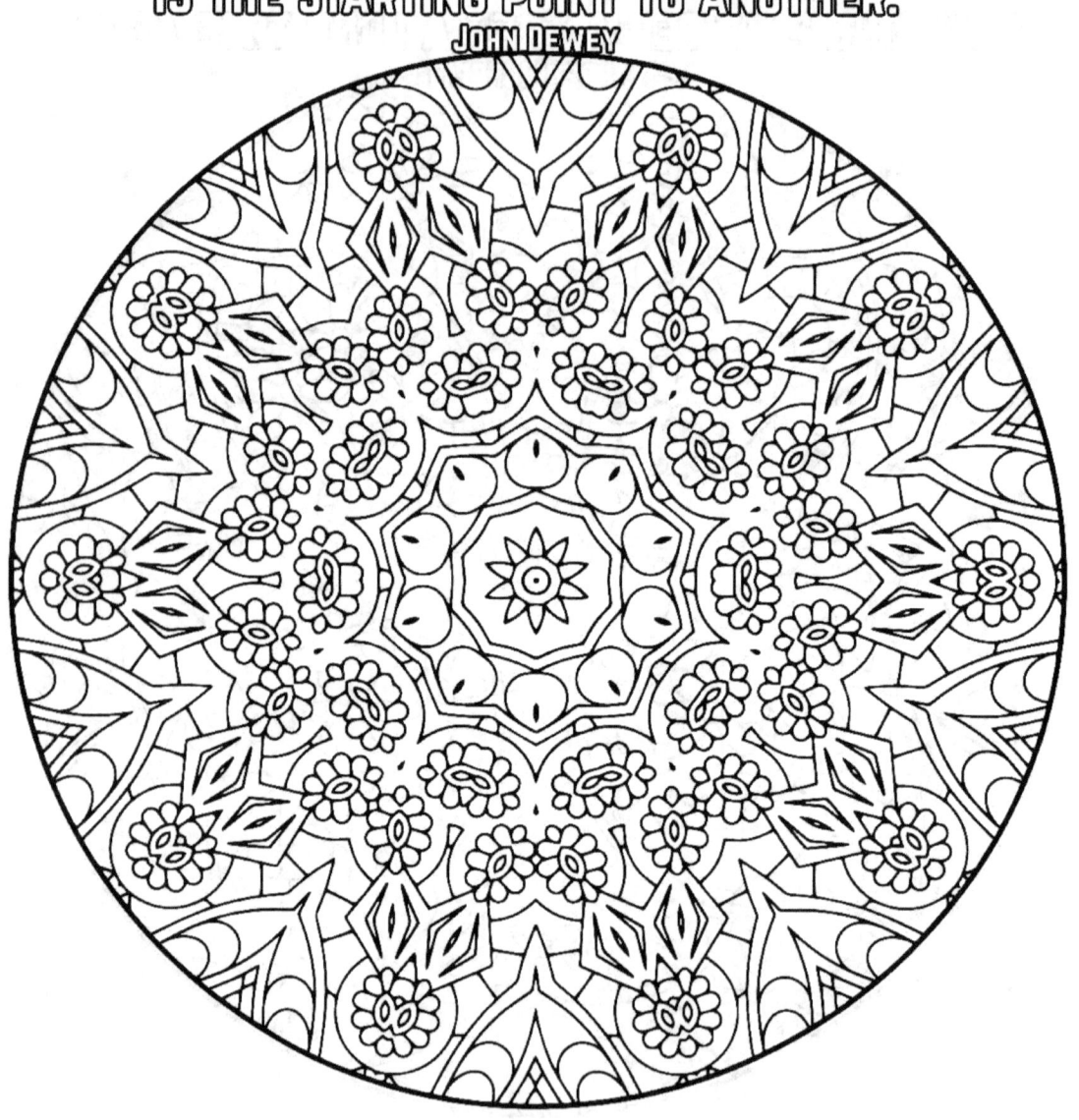

"COURAGE IS THE PRICE THAT LIFE EXACTS
FOR GRANTING PEACE."
AMELIA EARHART

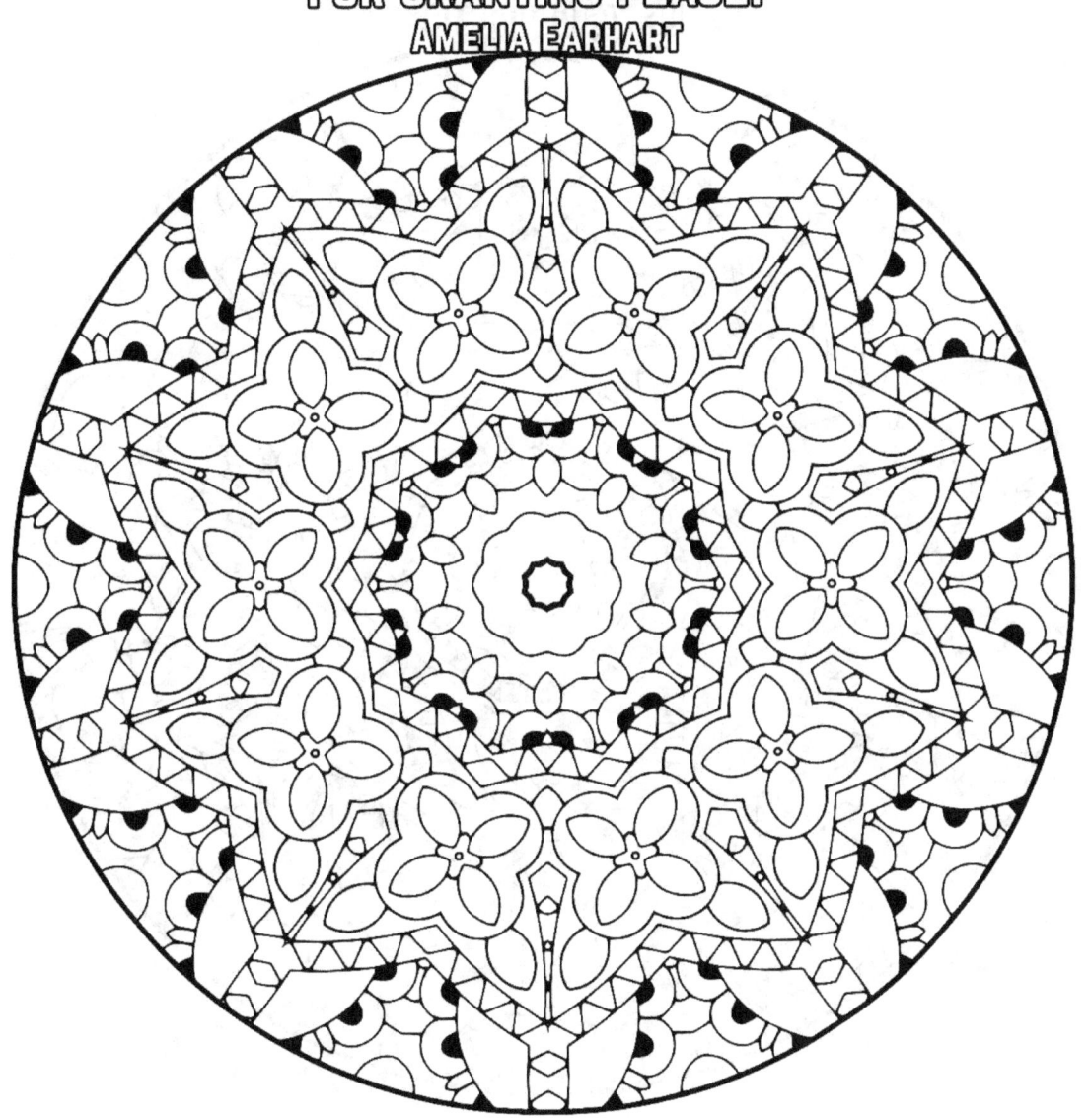

"THE LOFTY OAK FROM A SMALL ACORN GROWS."
LEWIS DUNCOMBE

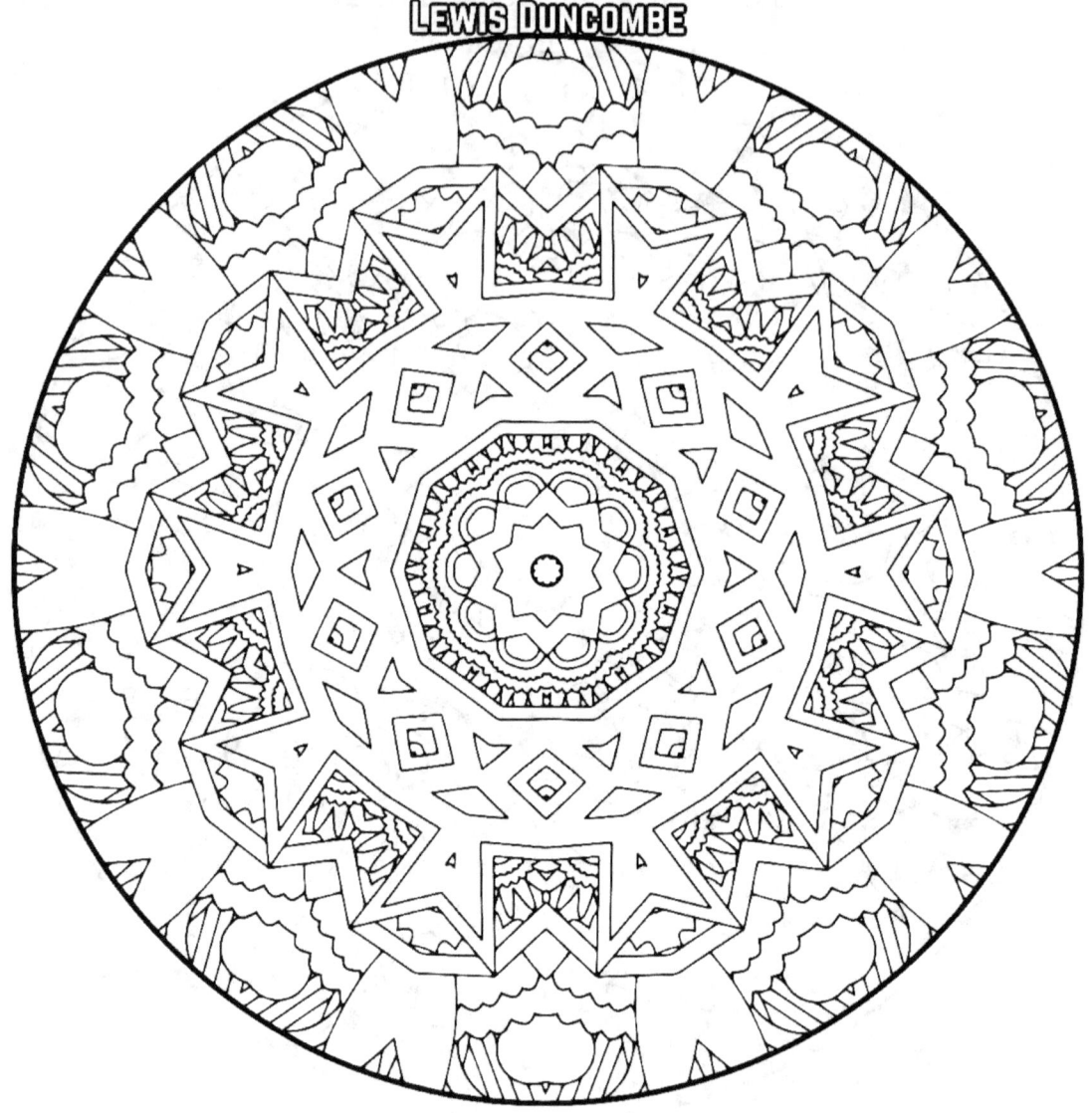

"GENIUS IS ONE PERCENT INSPIRATION
AND 99 PERCENT PERSPIRATION."
THOMAS EDISON

"LIFE'S TRAGEDY IS THAT WE GET OLD TO SOON
AND WISE TOO LATE."
BENJAMIN FRANKLIN

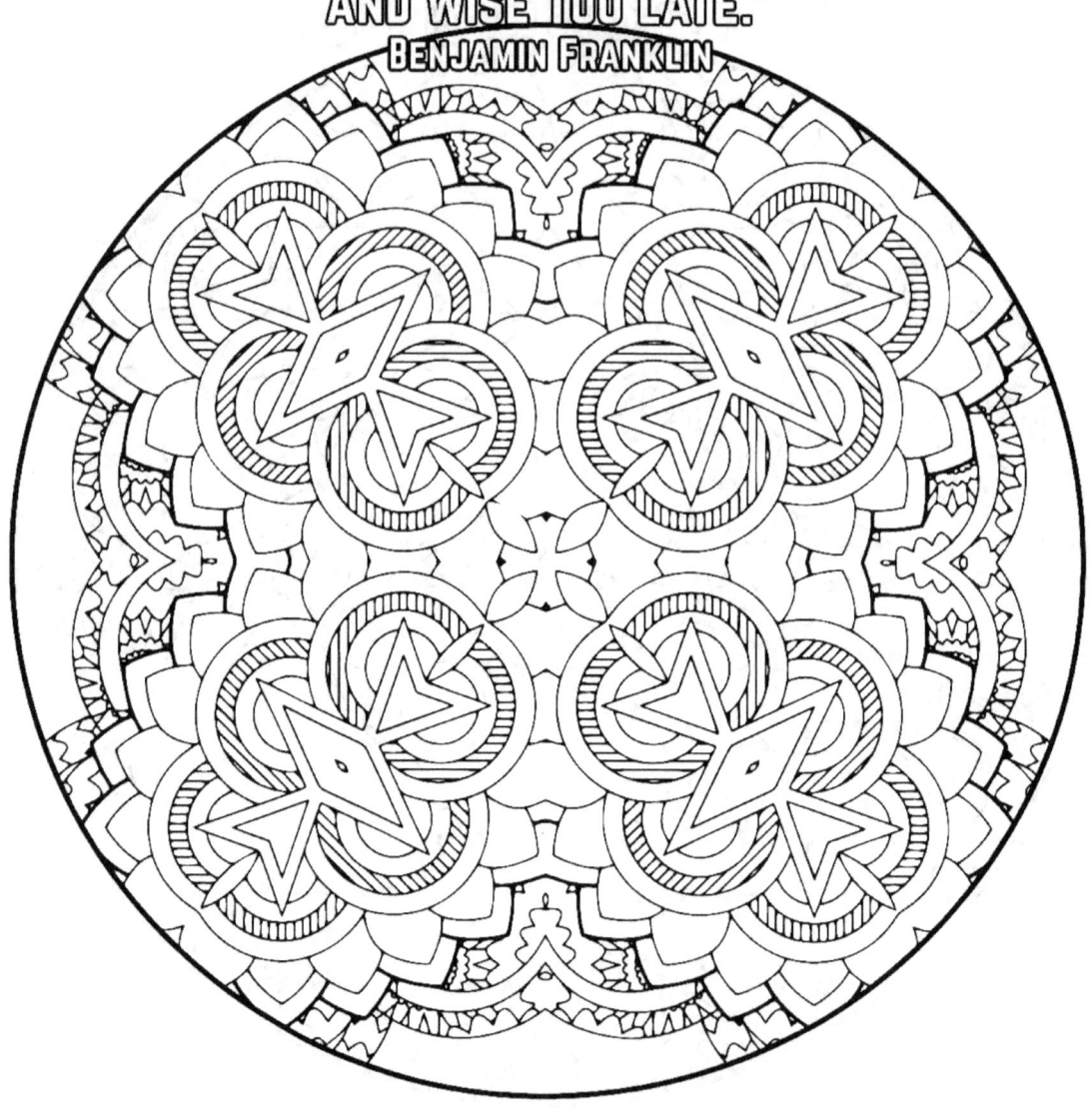

"YOU CAN ONLY LIVE ONCE,
BUT IF YOU LIVE RIGHT,
ONCE IS ENOUGH."
JOE E. LEWIS

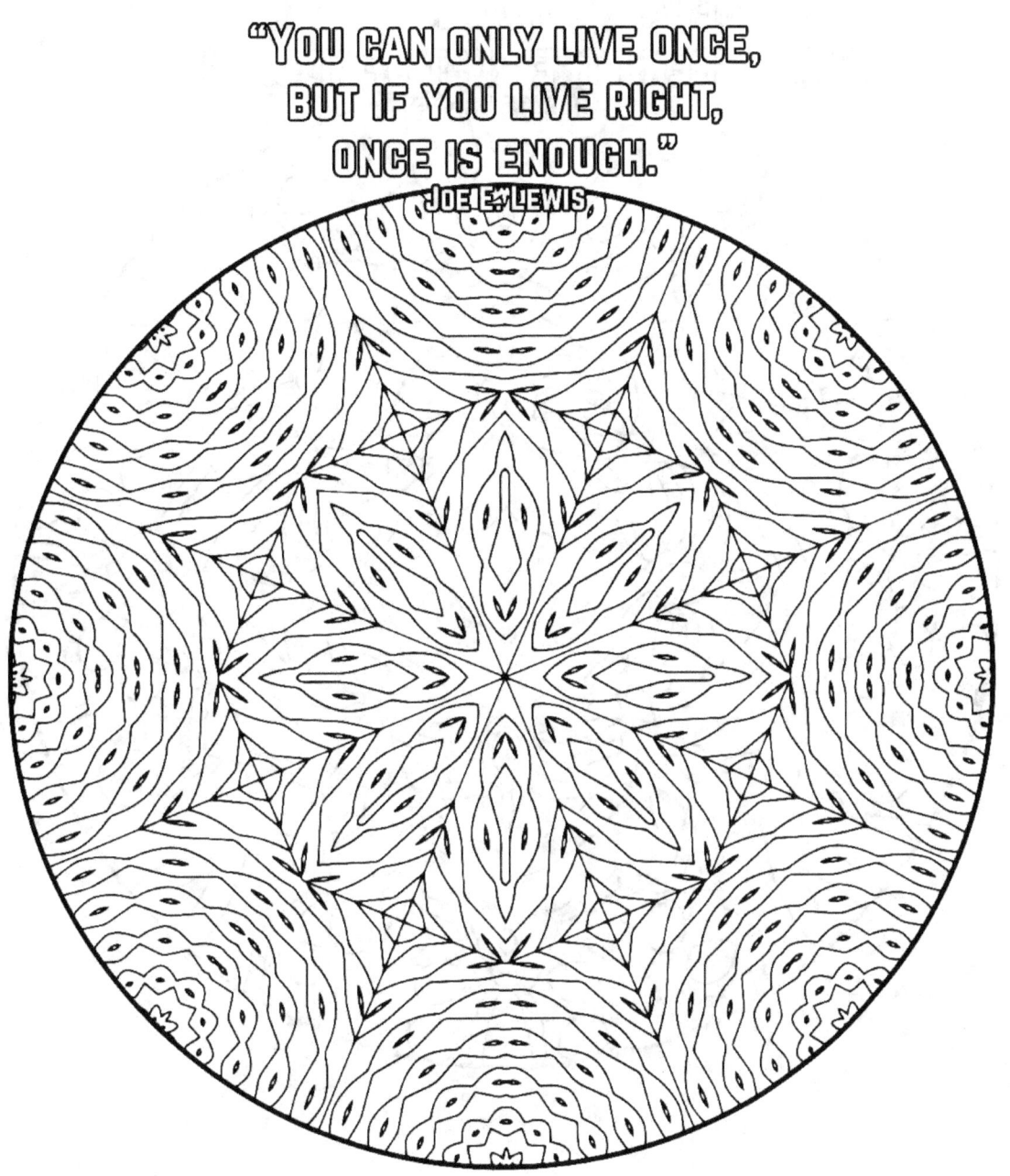

"LOOK TO THE FUTURE,
BECAUSE THAT IS WHERE
YOU'LL SPEND THE REST OF YOUR LIFE."
GEORGE BURNS

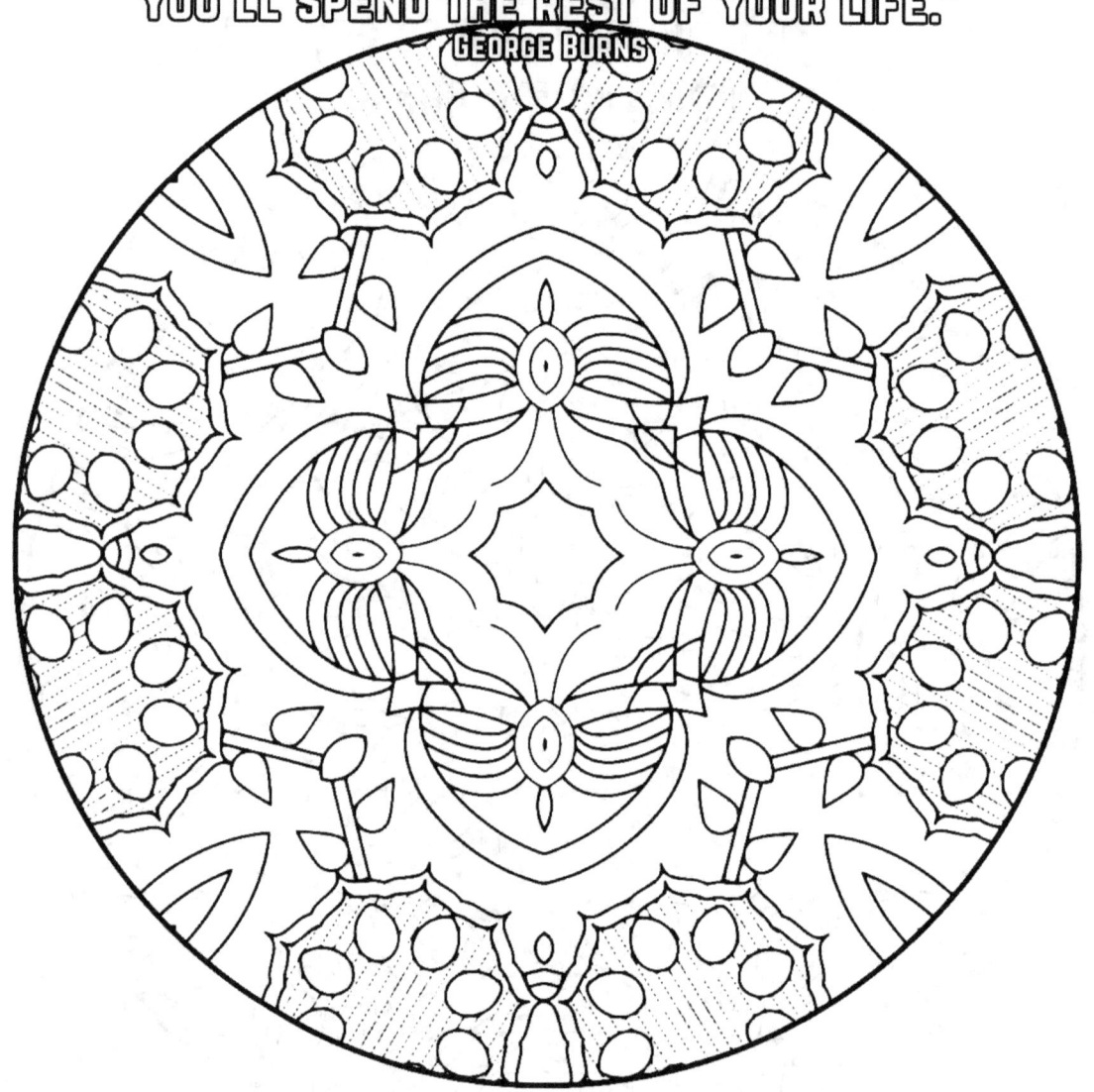

"AND IN THE END
IT'S NOT THE YEARS IN YOUR LIFE THAT COUNT.
IT'S THE LIFE IN YOUR YEARS."
ABRAHAM LINCOLN

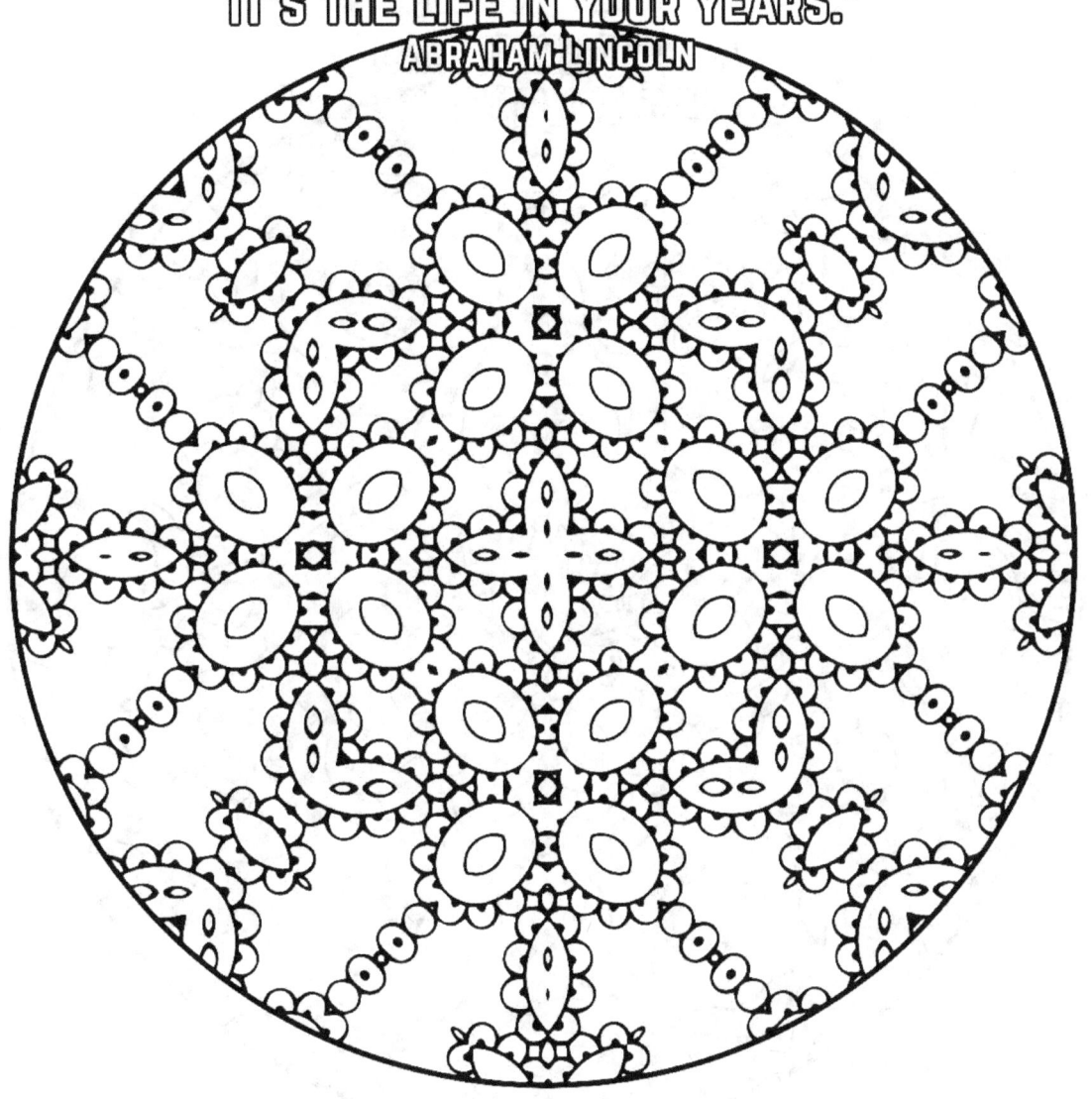

"BE TRUE TO YOUR WORK,
YOUR WORD,
AND YOUR FRIEND."
HENRY DAVID THOREAU

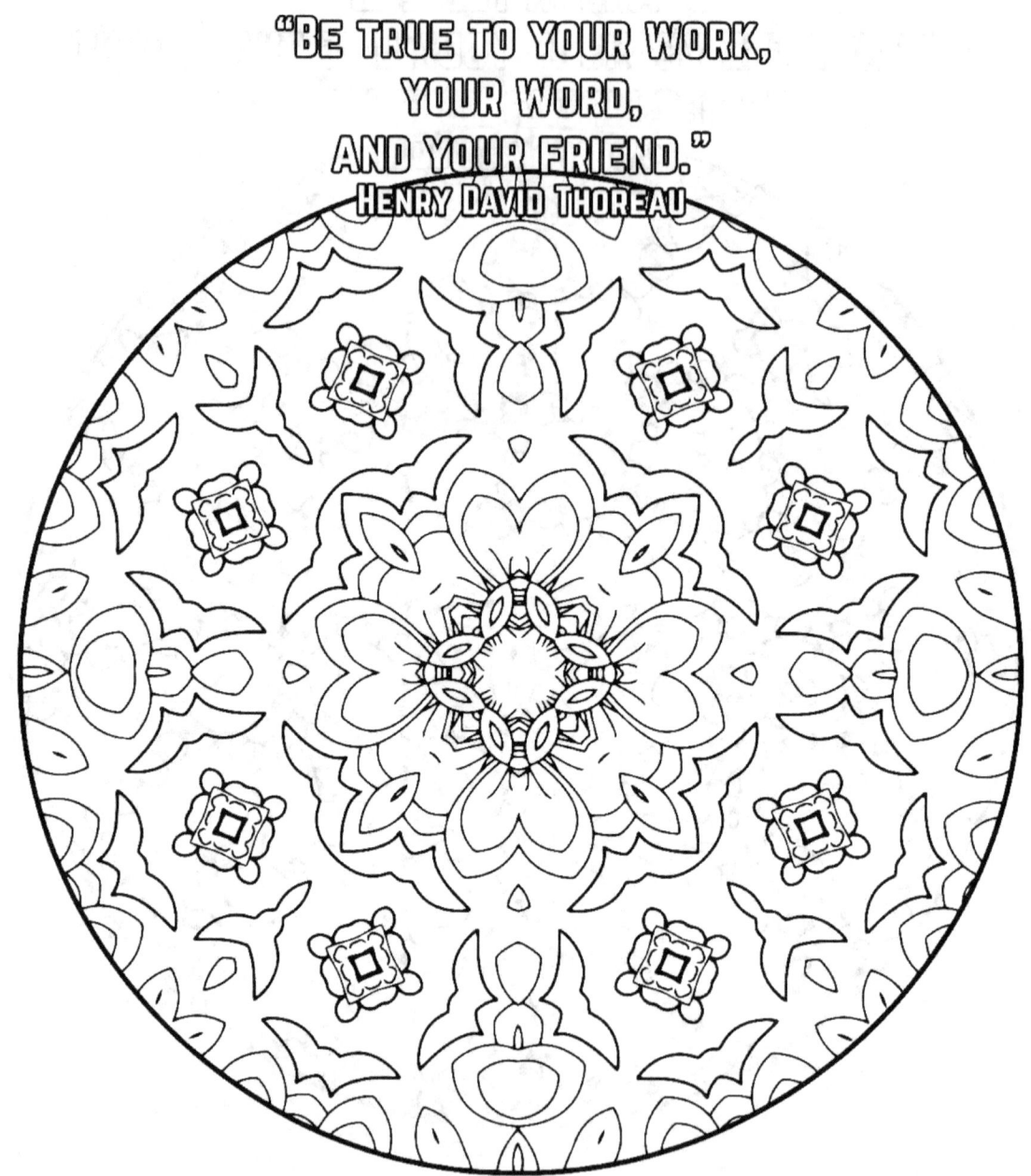

"I ALWAYS WANTED TO BE SOMEBODY,
BUT NOW I REALIZE
I SHOULD HAVE BEEN MORE SPECIFIC."
LILLY TOMLIN

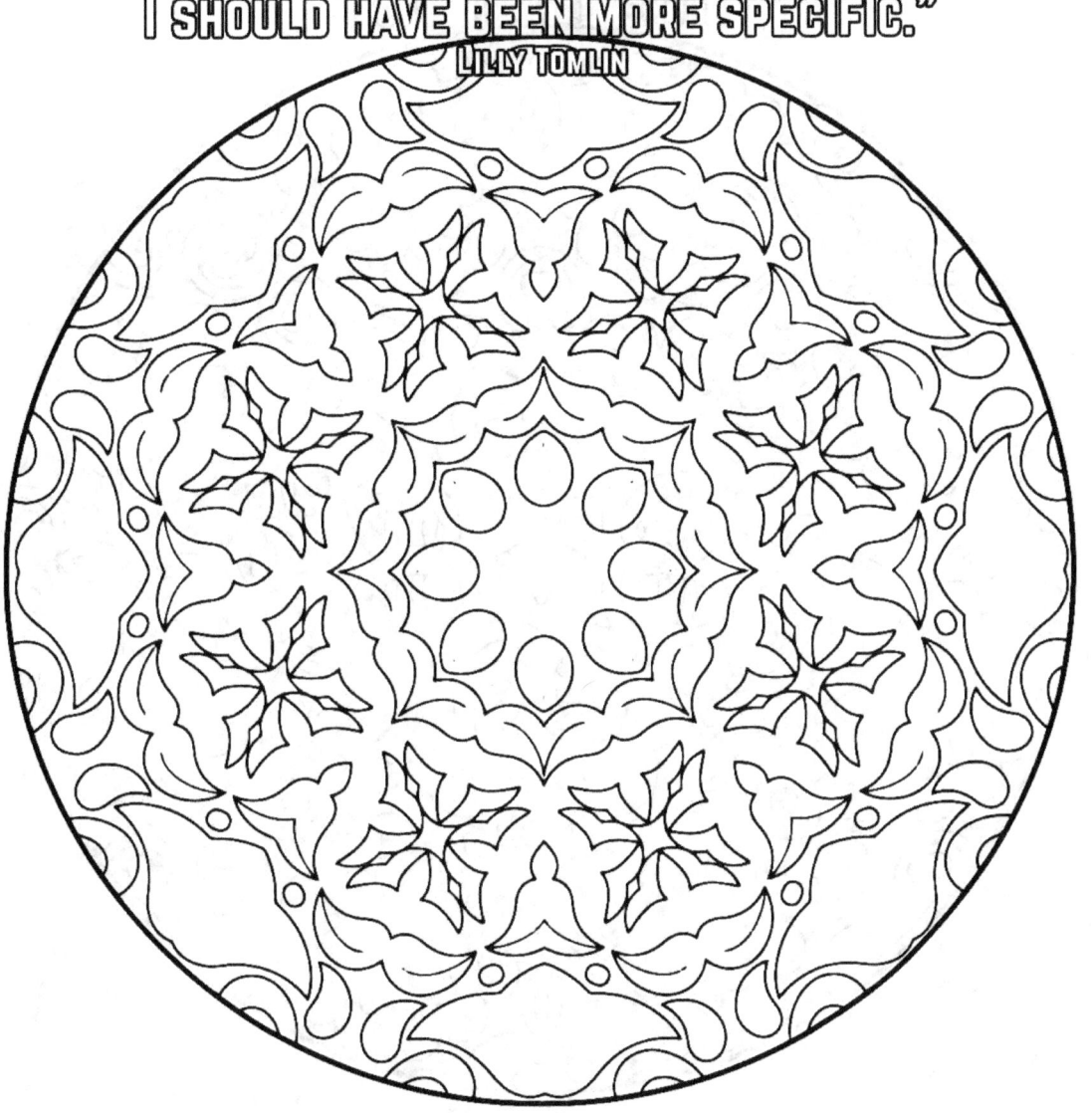

"CHARACTER, NOT CIRCUMSTANCE,
MAKES THE PERSON."
BOOKER T. WASHINGTON

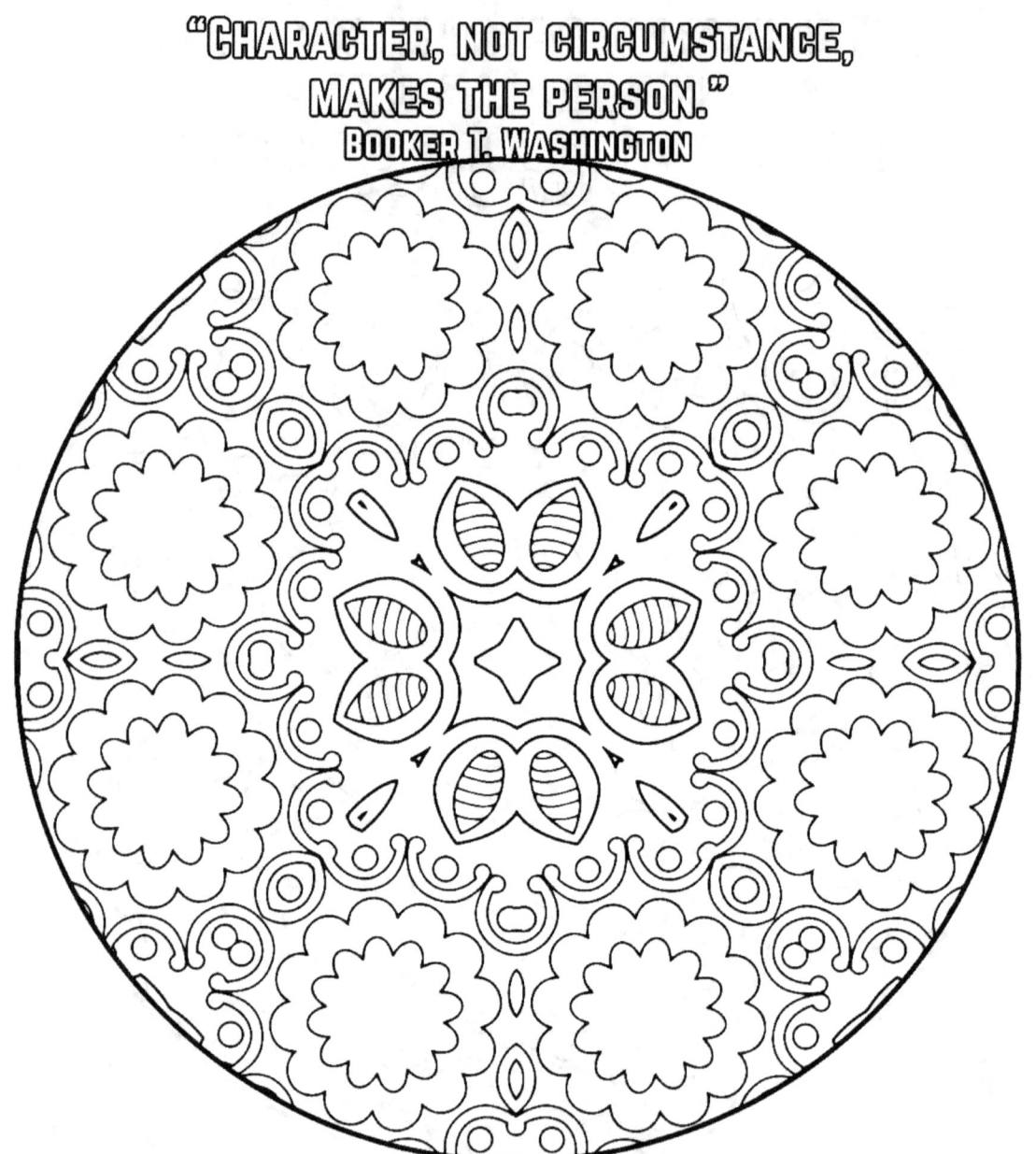

"EVERY MAN IS GUILTY
OF ALL THE GOOD HE DIDN'T DO."
VOLTAIRE

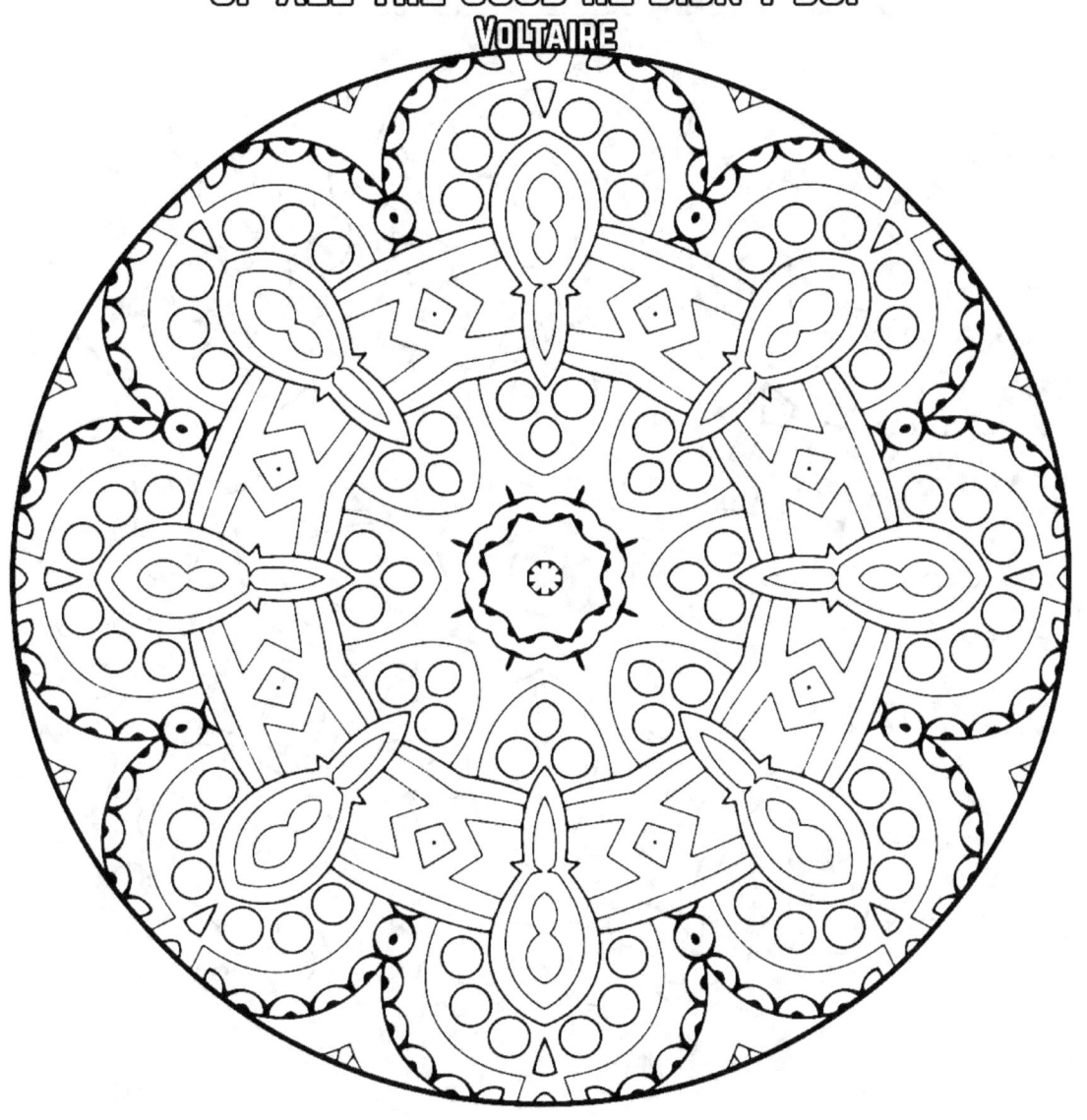

"IF LIFE WERE MEASURED BY ACCOMPLISHMENTS,
MOST OF US WOULD DIE IN INFANCY."
A. P. GOUTHEY

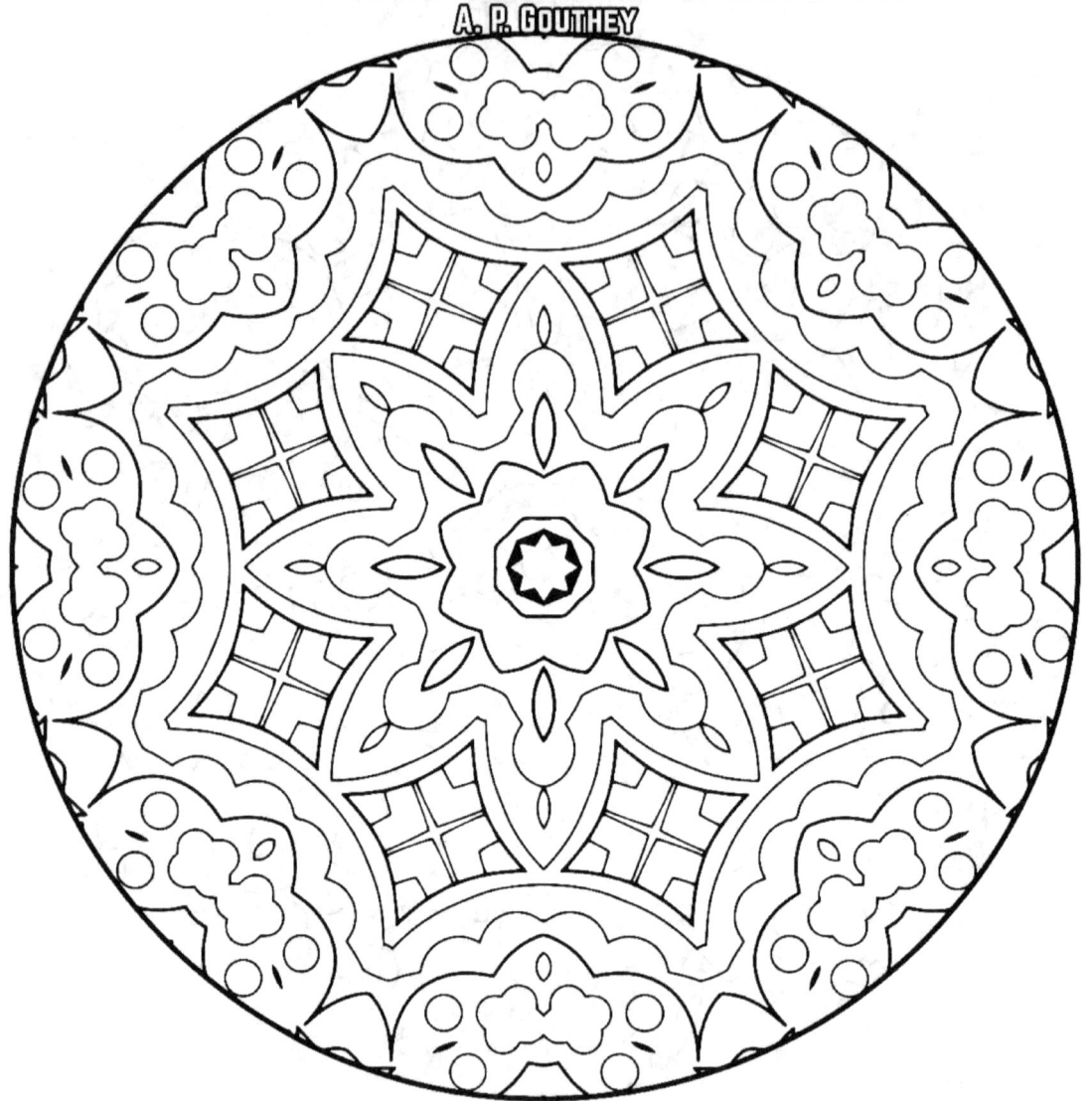

"WE WILL EITHER FIND A WAY,
OR MAKE ONE."
HANNIBAL

"IT DOES NOT MATTER HOW SLOWLY YOU GO
SO LONG AS YOU DO NOT STOP."
CONFUCIUS

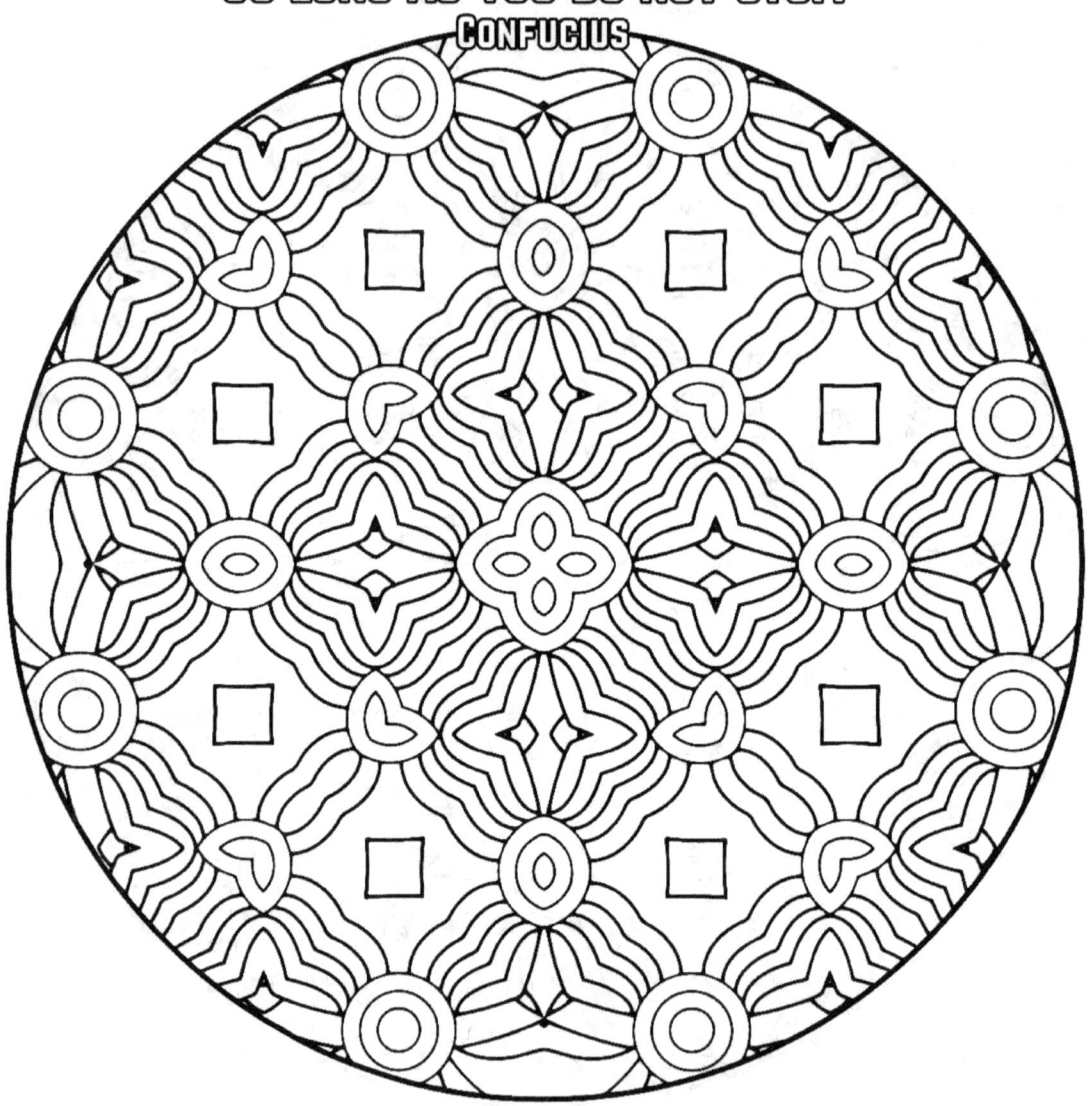

"IF YOU CHASE TWO RABBITS,
BOTH WILL ESCAPE."
CHINESE PROVERB

"IT IS A MISTAKE TO TRY TO LOOK TOO FAR AHEAD.
THE CHAIN OF DESTINY CAN ONLY BE GRASPED
ONE LINK AT A TIME."
WINSTON CHURCHILL

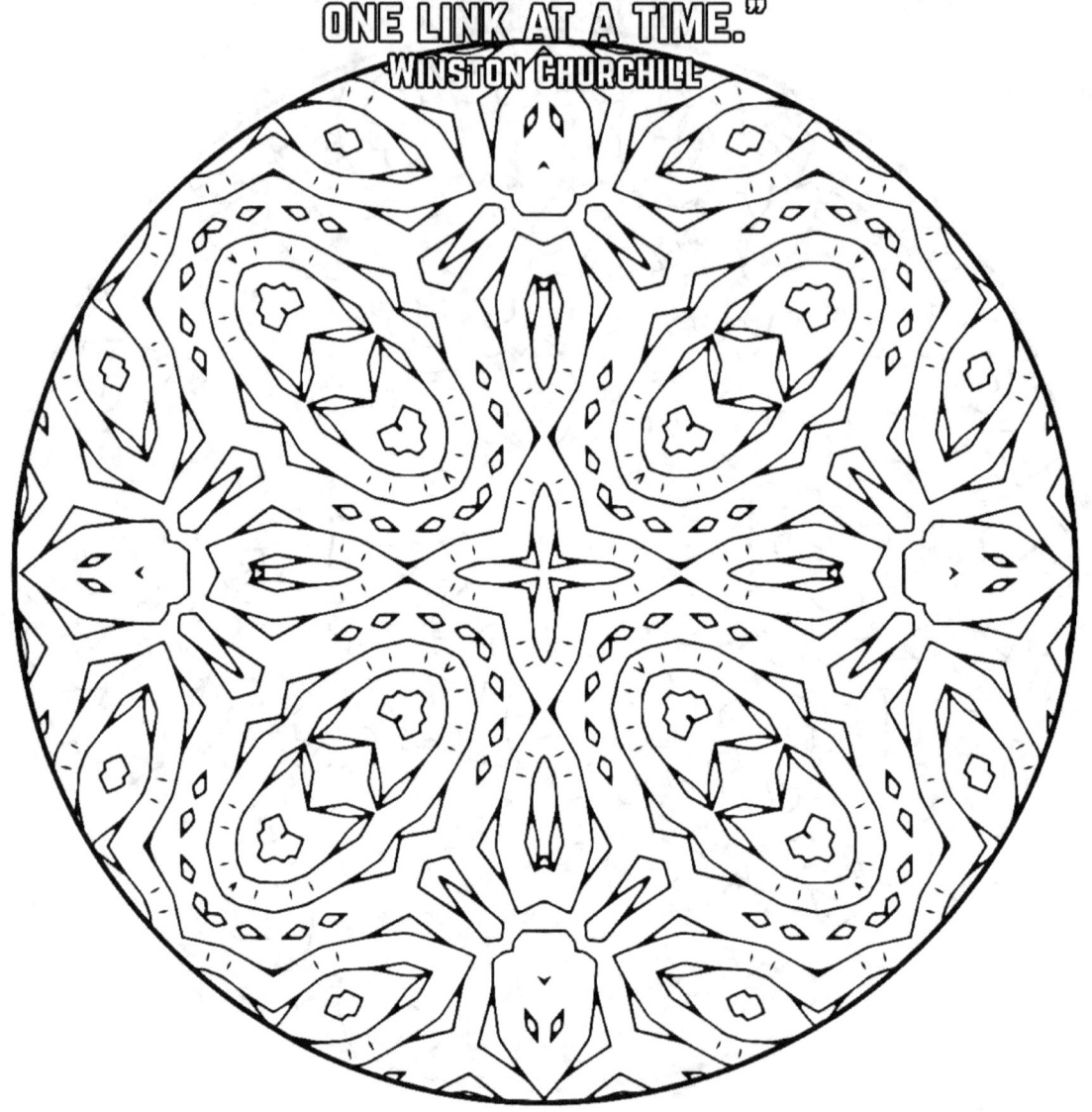

"BE THE CHANGE YOU WANT TO SEE IN THE WORLD."
MAHATMA GANDHI

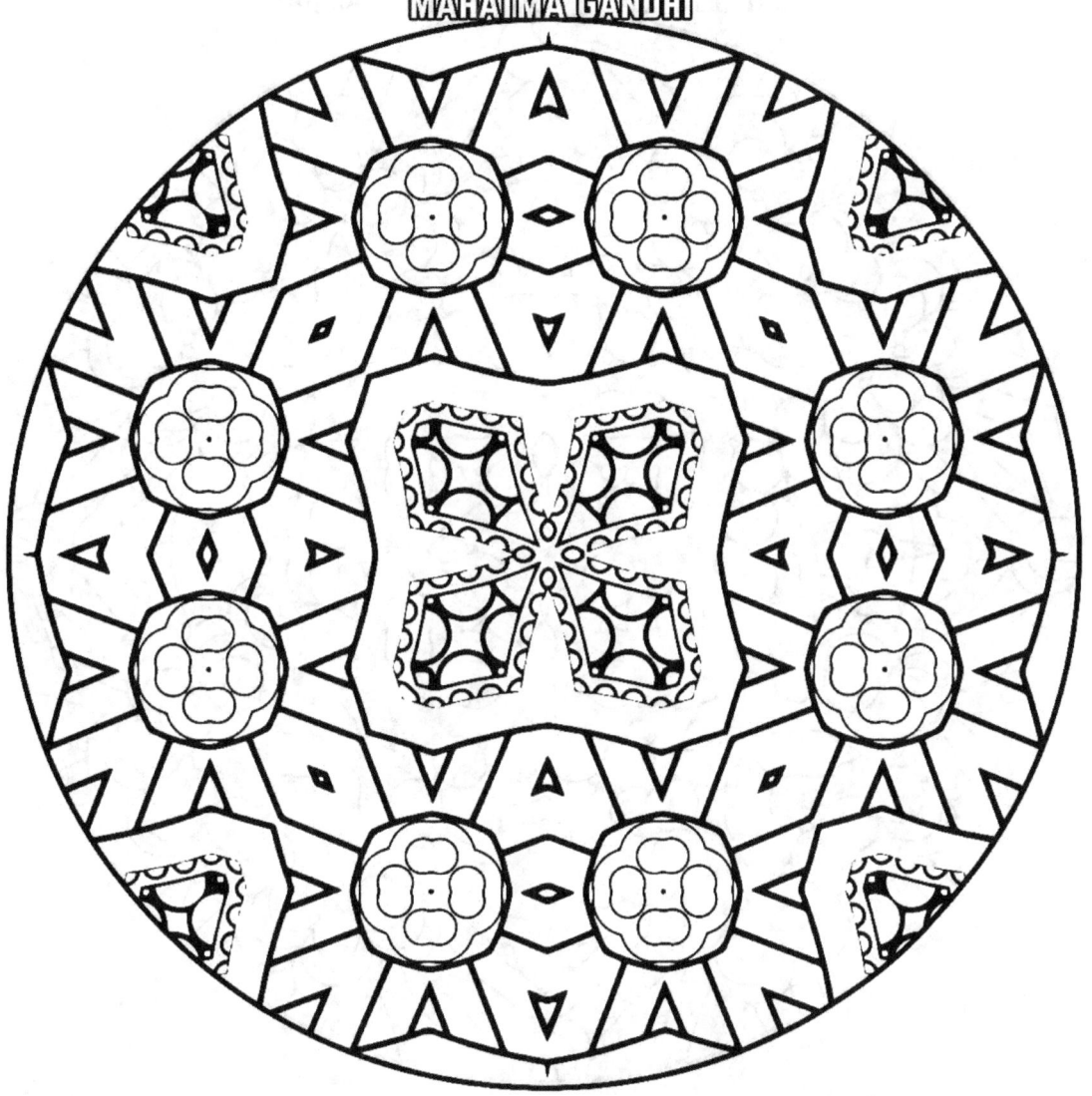

"A USELESS LIFE IS AN EARLY DEATH."
JOHANN WOLFGANG VON GOETHE

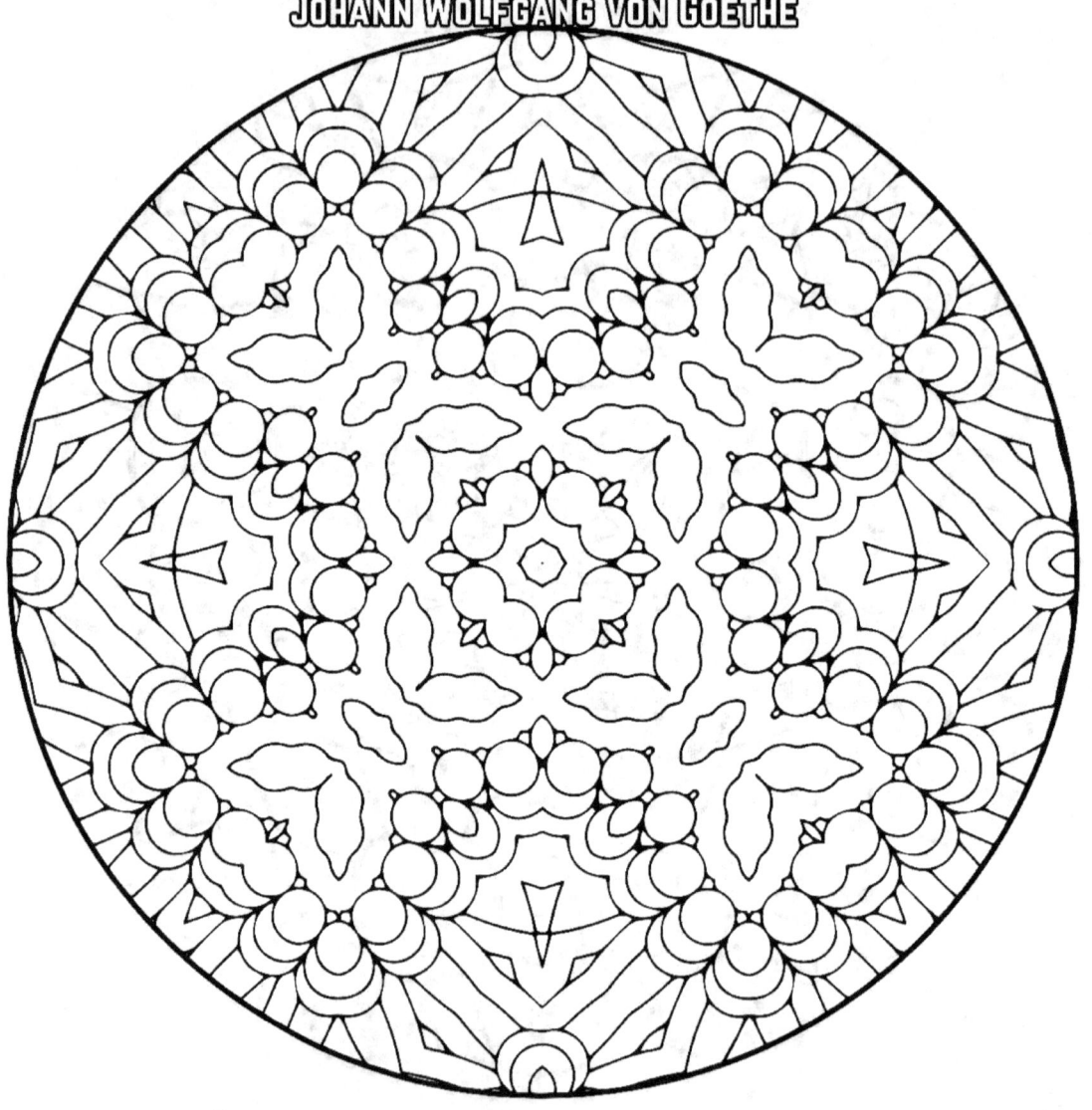

"KEEP YOUR FACE TO THE SUNSHINE
AND YOU CANNOT SEE THE SHADOW."
HELEN KELLER

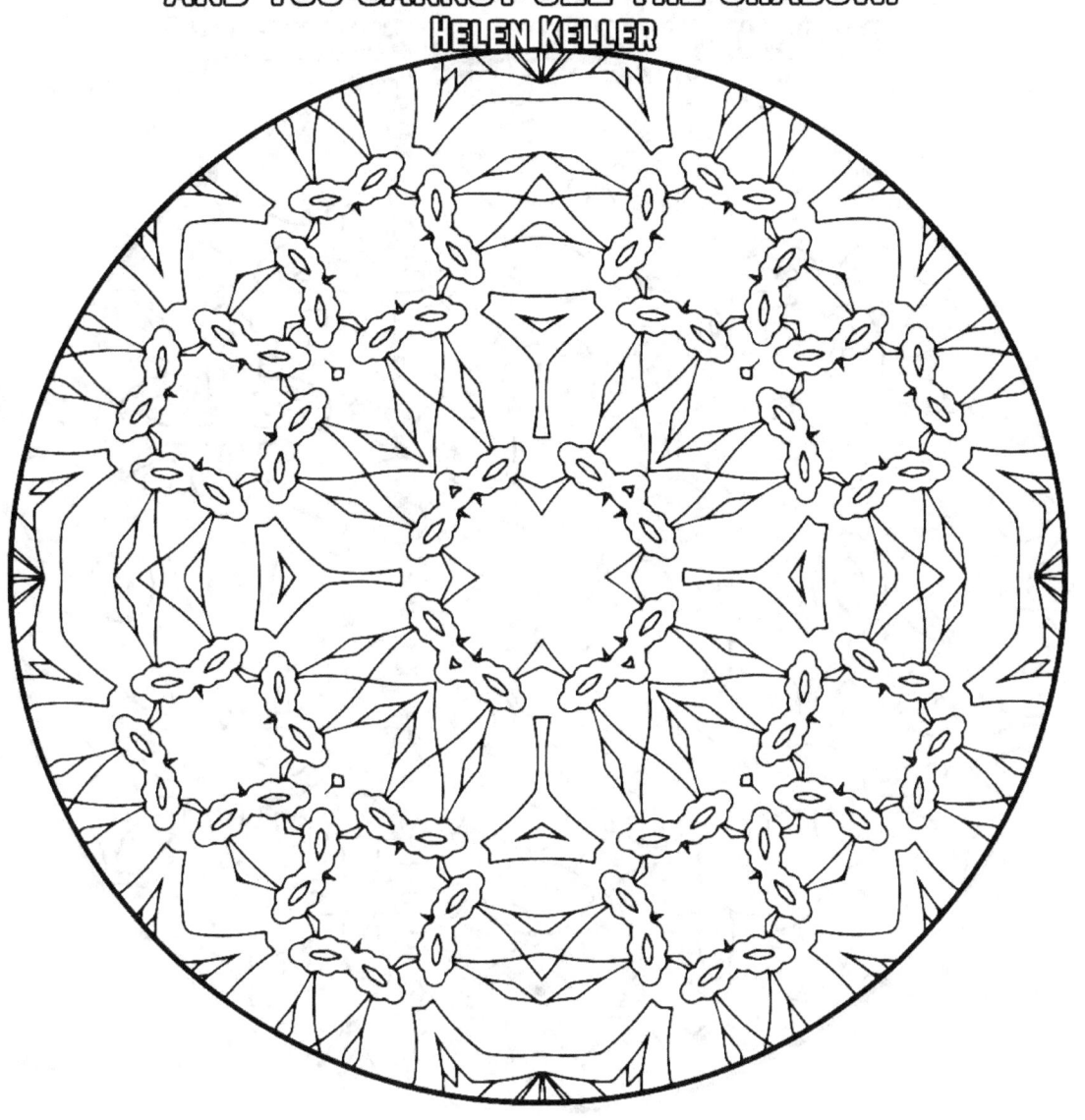

"WHEN YOU ARE RIGHT, YOU CANNOT BE TOO RADICAL;
WHEN YOU ARE WRONG,
YOU CANNOT BE TOO CONSERVATIVE."
MARTIN LUTHER KING, JR.

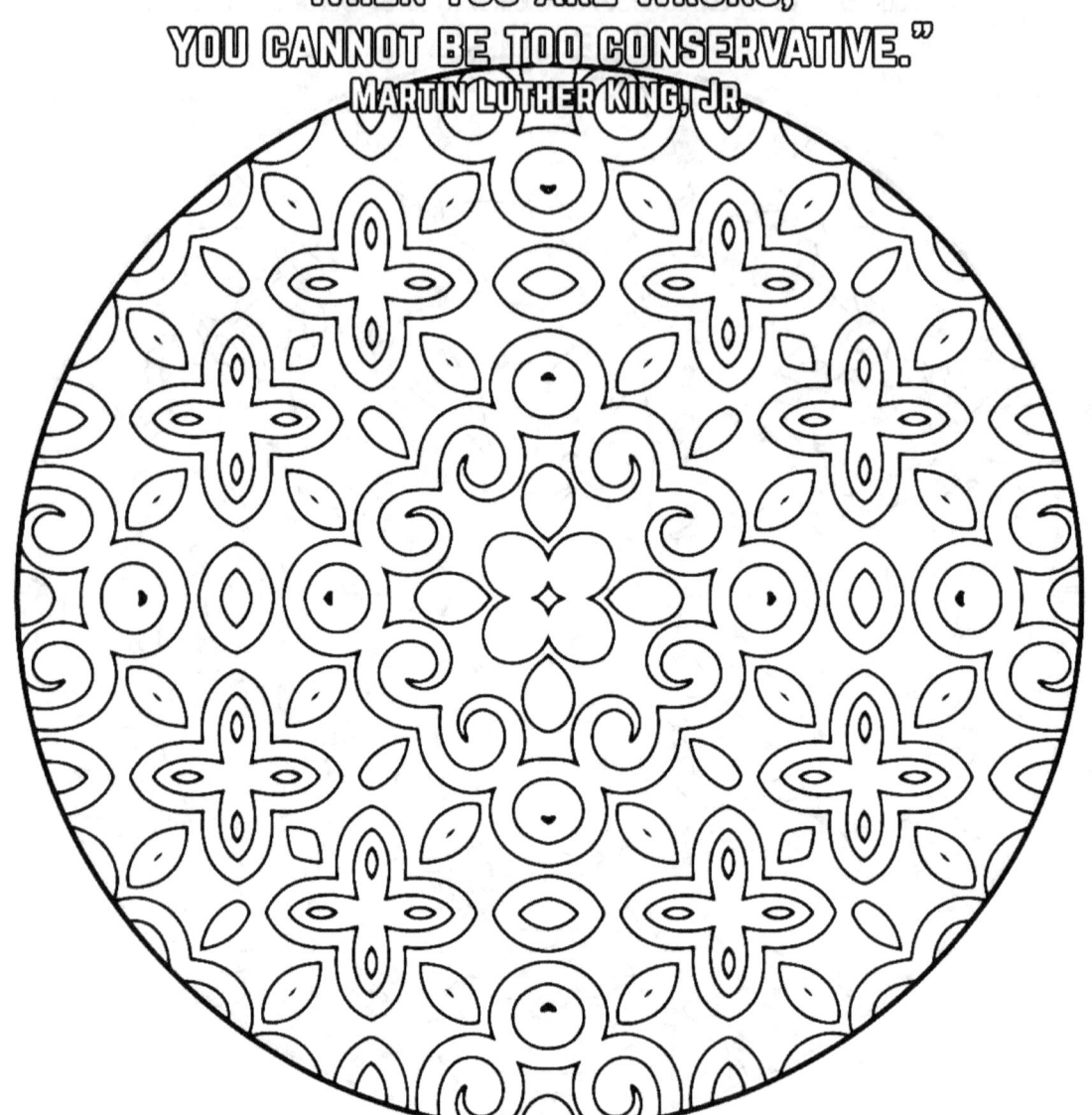

"I BELIEVE DEEPLY THAT WE MUST FIND,
ALL OF US TOGETHER,
A NEW SPIRITUALITY."
DALAI LAMA

"THE REAL VOYAGE OF DISCOVERY
CONSISTS NOT IN SEEKING NEW LANDSCAPES,
BUT IN HAVING NEW EYES."
MARCEL PROUST

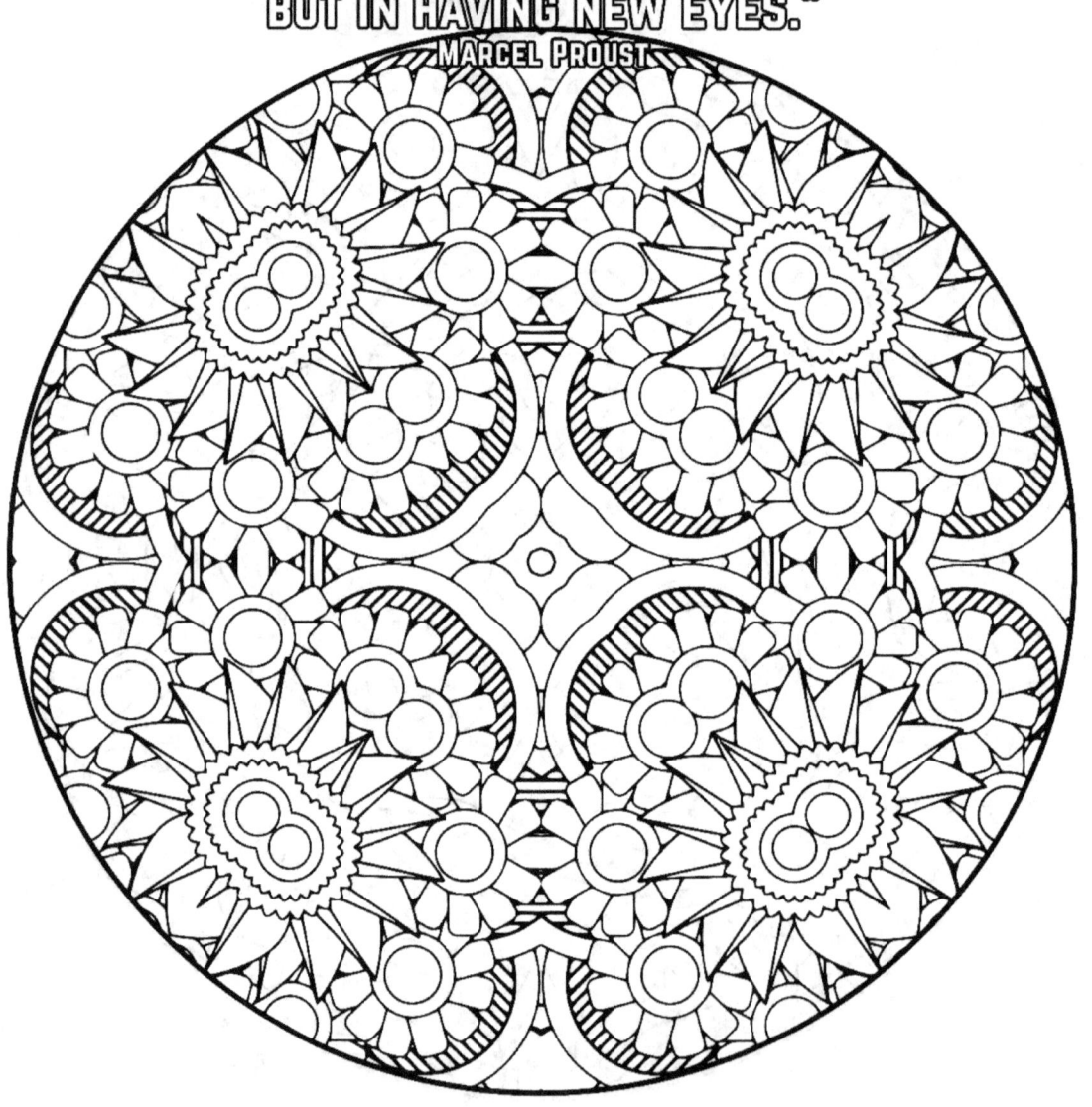

"THE FUTURE BELONGS TO THOSE WHO BELIEVE
IN THE BEAUTY OF THEIR DREAMS."
ELEANOR ROOSEVELT

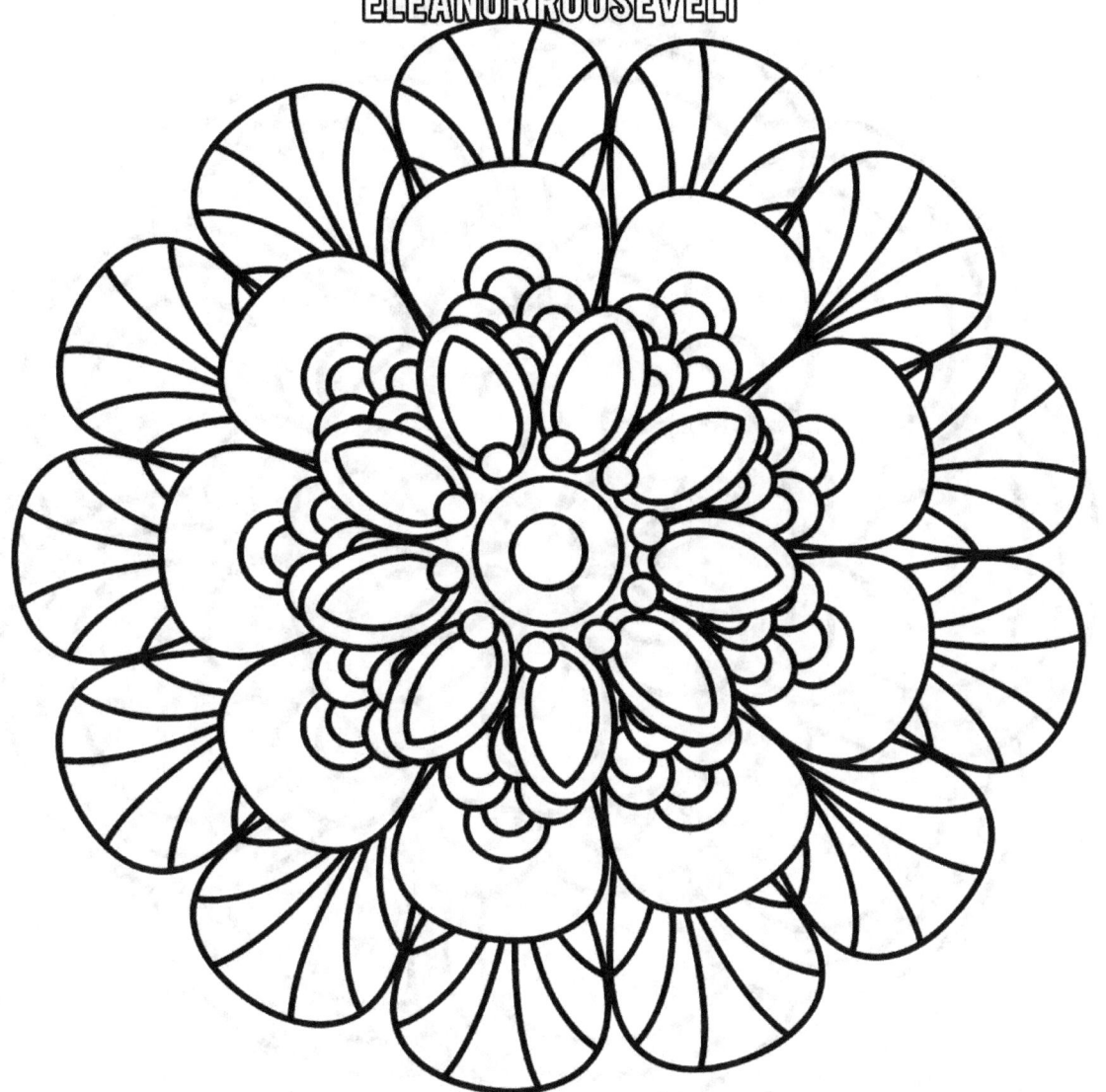

"INDIVIDUALLY, WE ARE ONE DROP.
TOGETHER, WE ARE AN OCEAN."
RYUNOSUKE SATORO

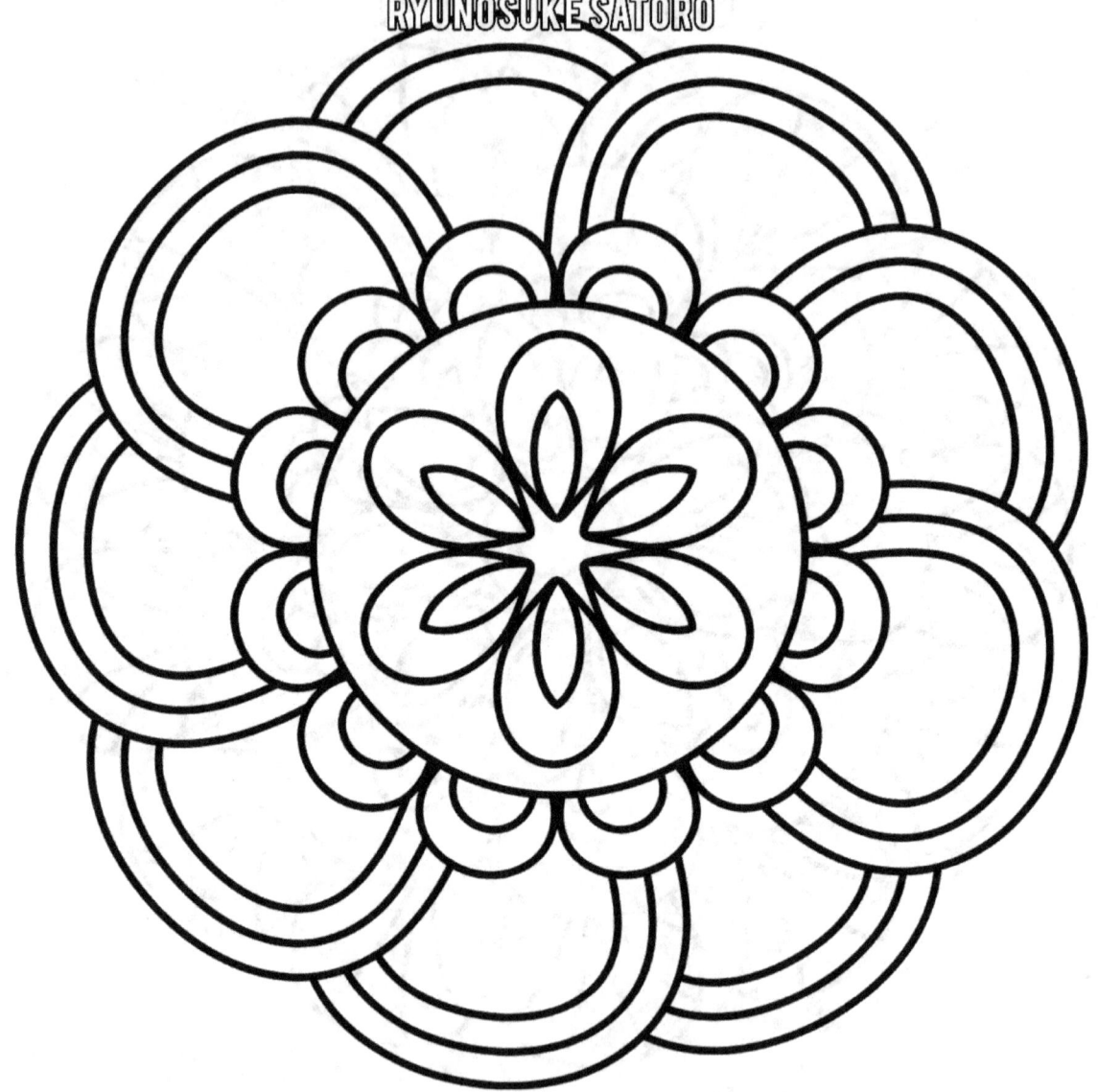

"NOTHING HAPPENS
UNLESS FIRST A DREAM."
CARL SANDBURG

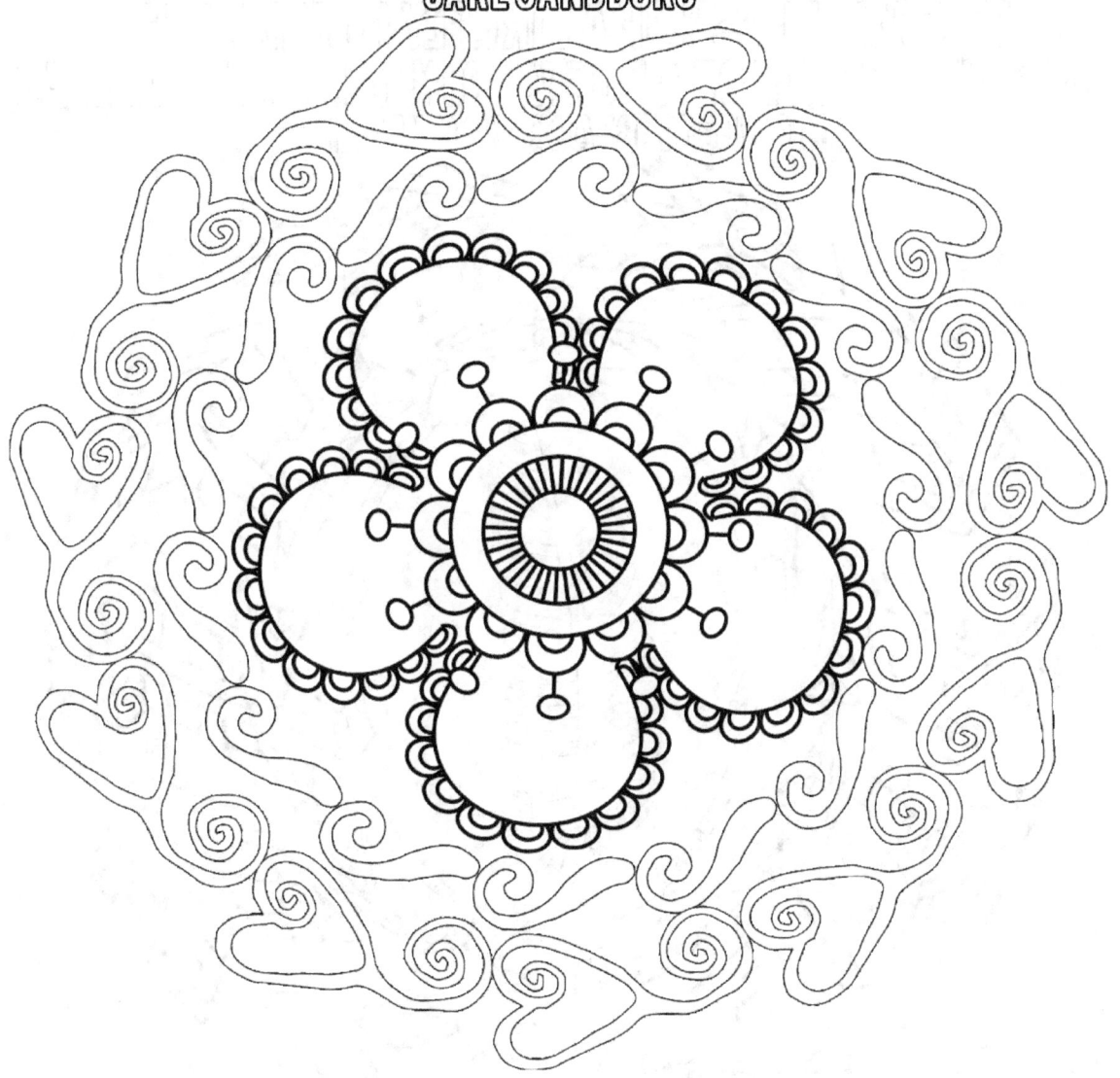

"WHAT IS LIFE?
IT IS THE FLASH OF A FIREFLY IN THE NIGHT.
IT IS THE BREATH OF A BUFFALO IN THE WINTERTIME."
CROWFOOT, BLACKFOOT WARRIOR

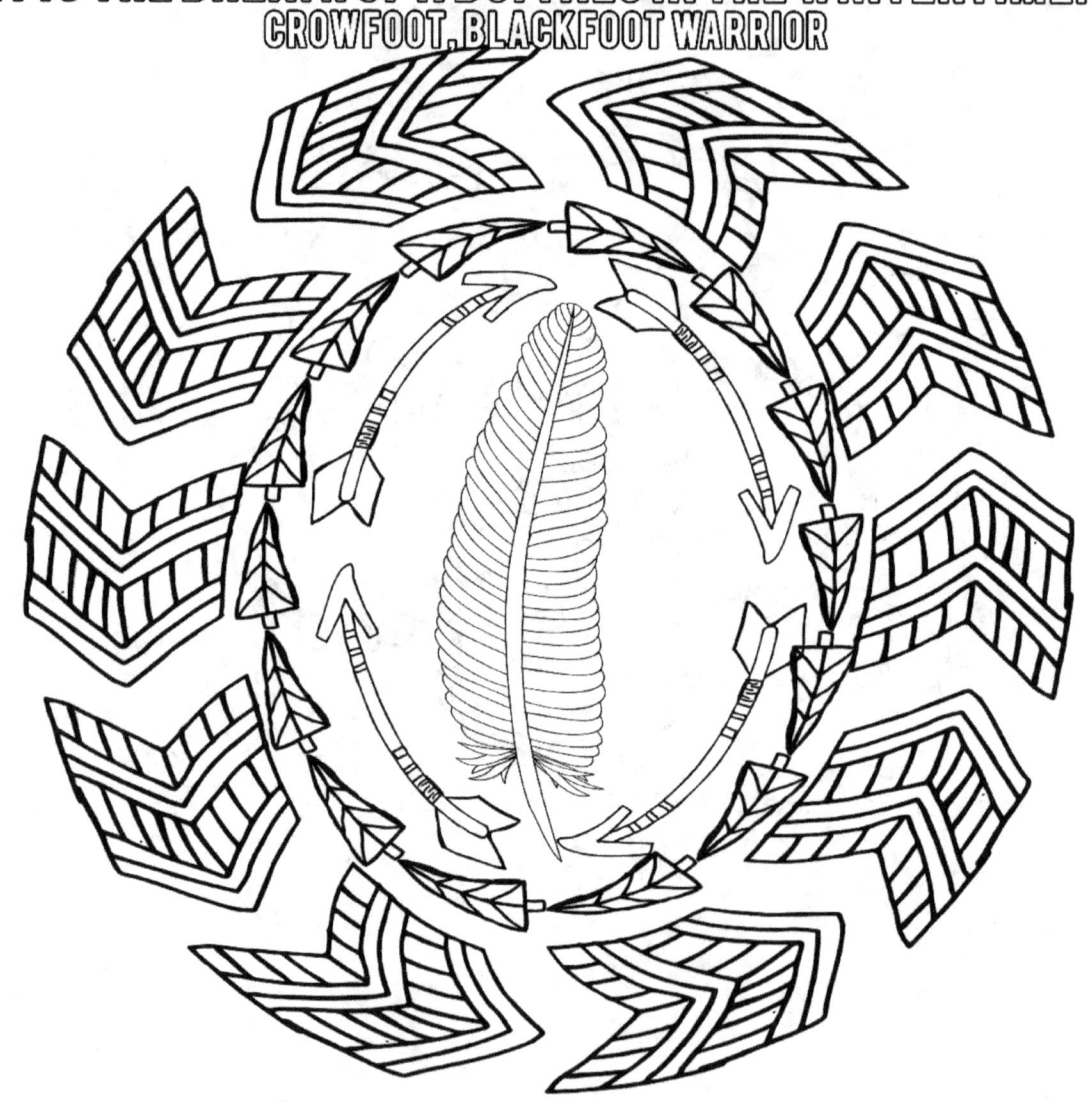

"GIVE EVERY MAN THY EAR, BUT FEW THY VOICE."
WILLIAM SHAKESPEARE

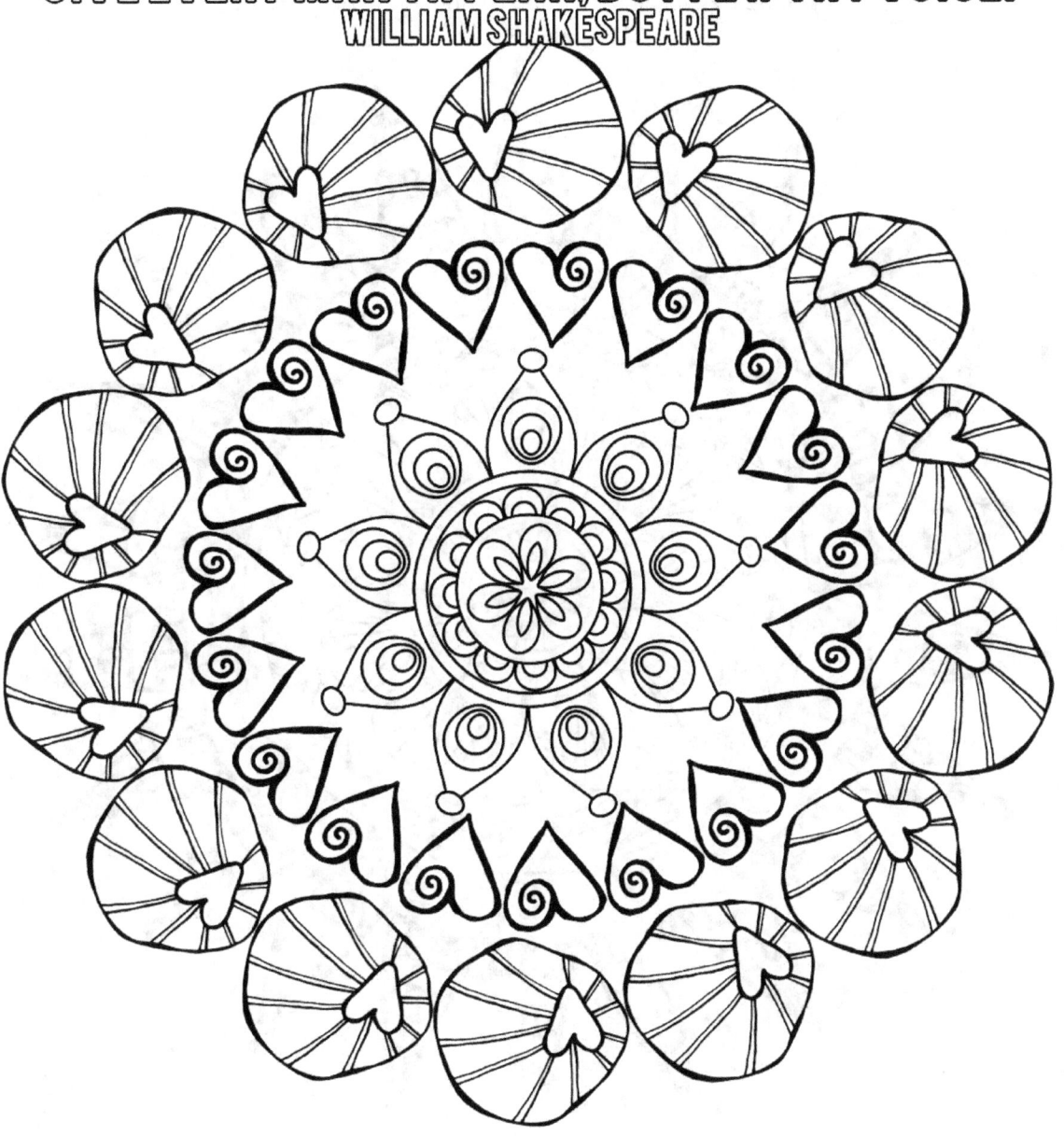

"WISDOM BEGINS IN WONDER."
SOCRATES

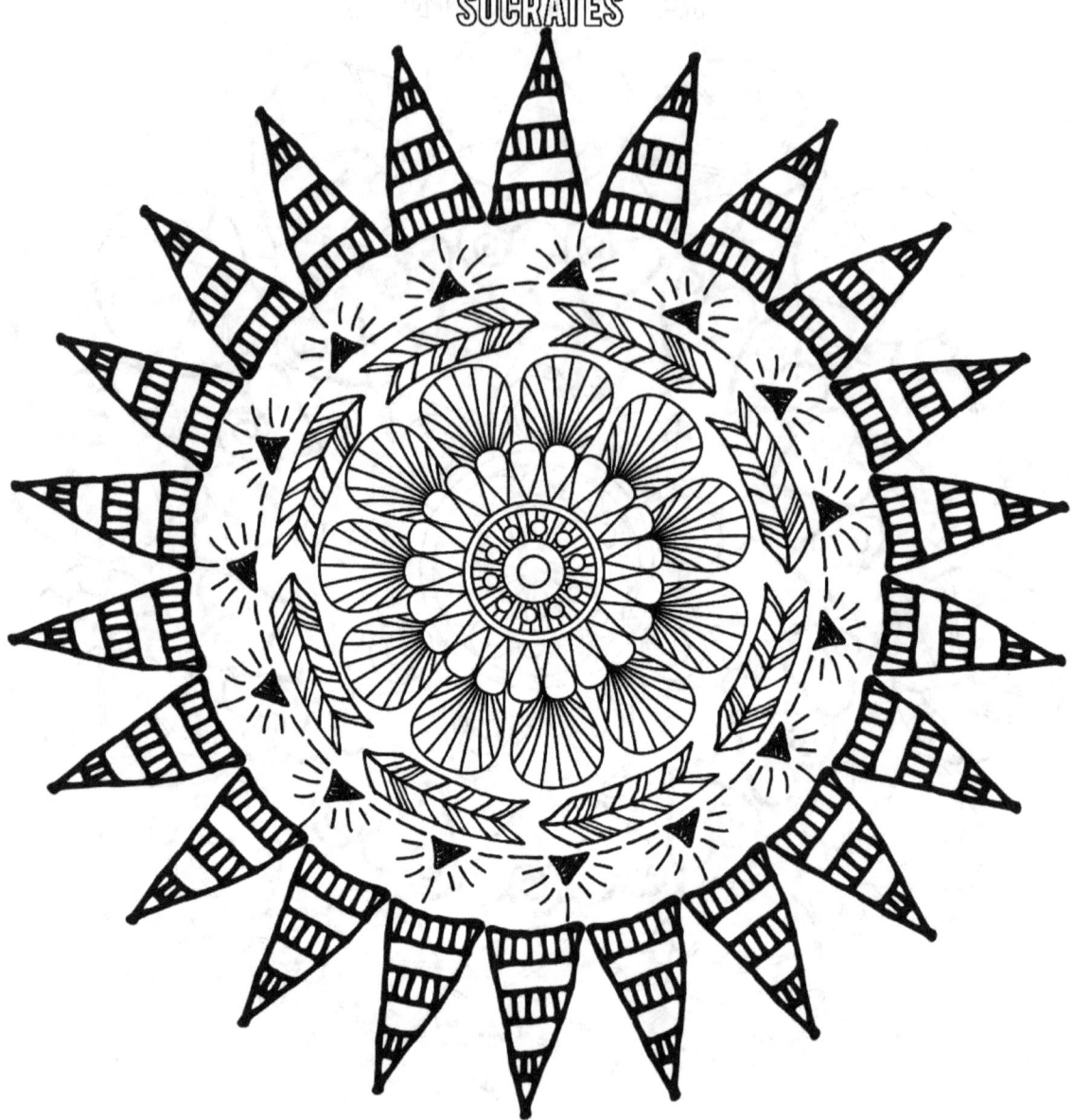

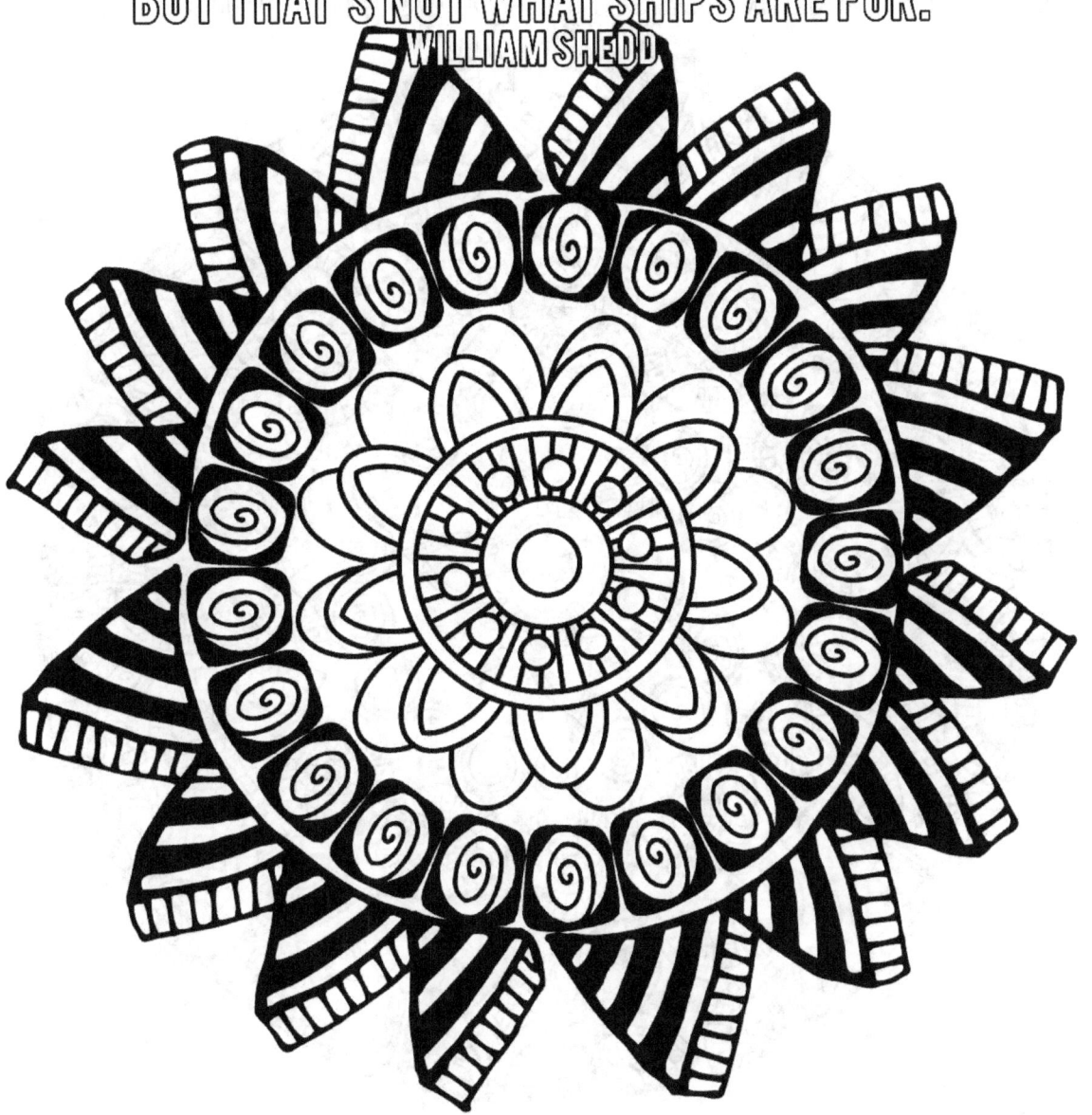

"A SHIP IS SAFE IN HARBOR,
BUT THAT'S NOT WHAT SHIPS ARE FOR."
WILLIAM SHEDD

"IF I HAVE SEEN FURTHER THAN OTHERS,
IT IS BY STANDING UPON THE SHOULDERS OF GIANTS."
ISAAC NEWTON

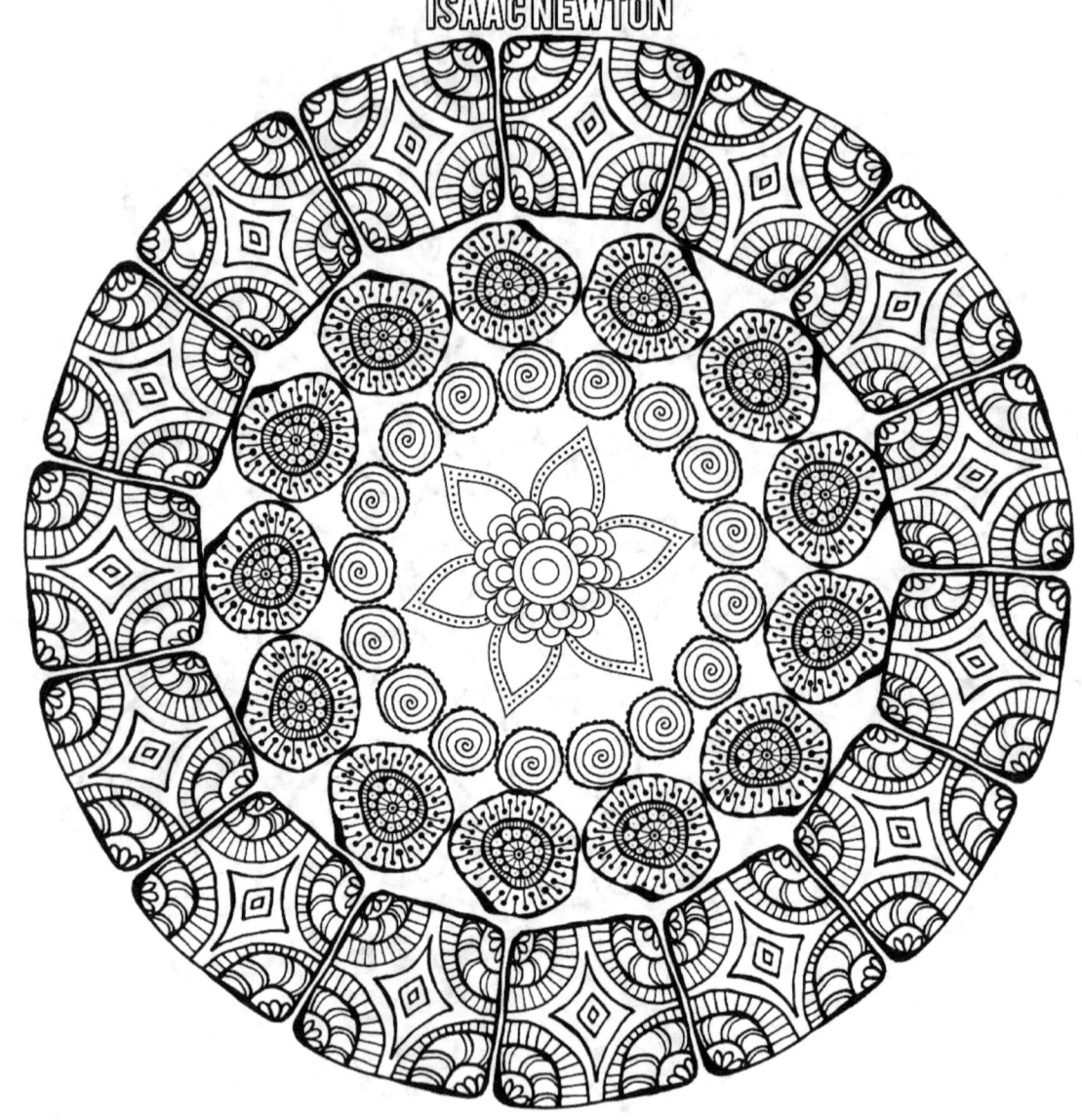

"TIME IS THE MOST VALUABLE THING
A MAN CAN SPEND."
HEOPHRASTUS

"SPECTACULAR ACHIEVEMENT IS ALWAYS PRECEDED BY UNSPECTACULAR PREPARATION."
ROBERT H. SCHULLER

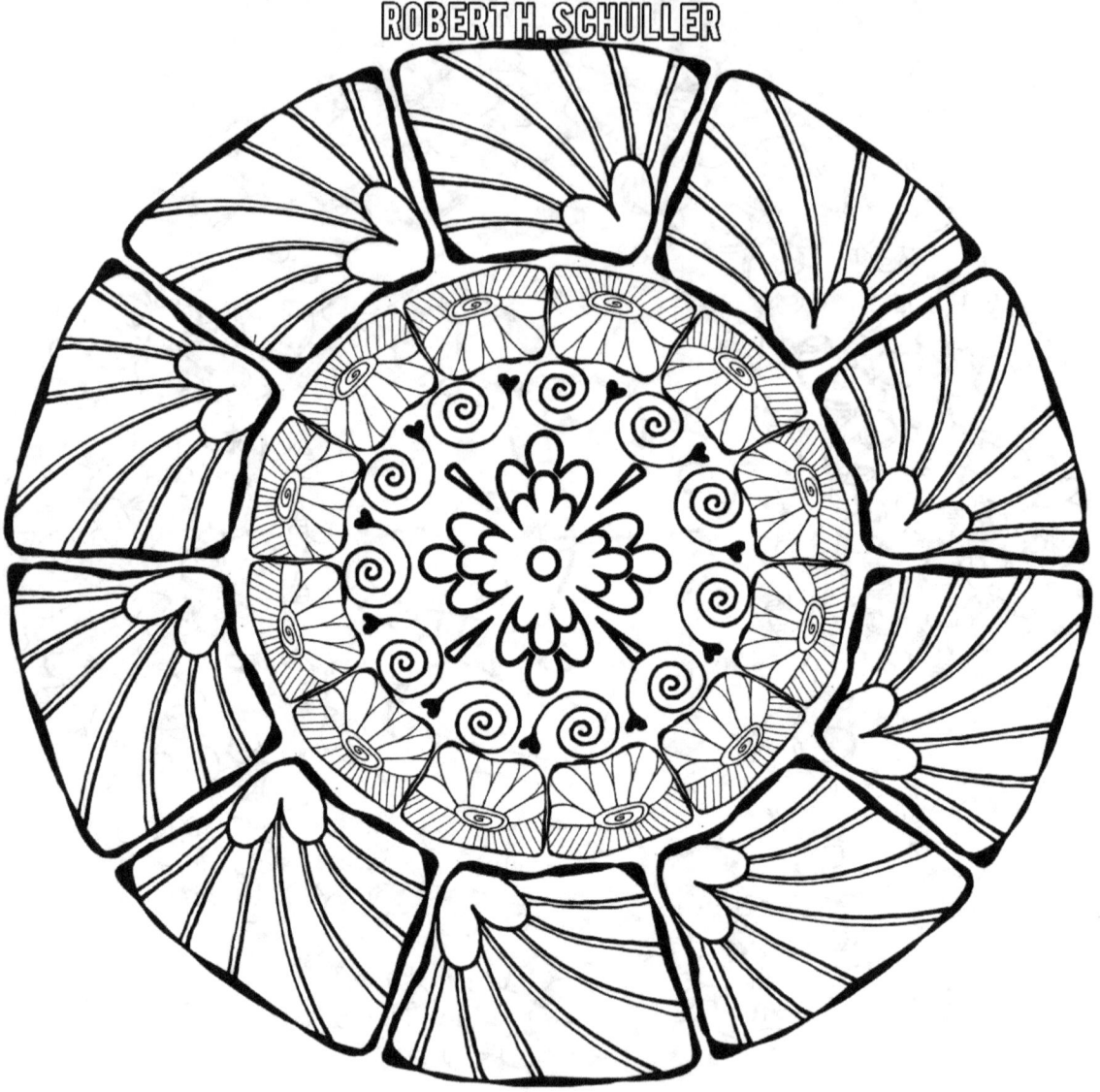

"LIFE IS LIKE A DOGSLED TEAM. IF YOU AIN'T THE LEAD DOG, THE SCENERY NEVER CHANGES."
LEWIS GRIZZARD

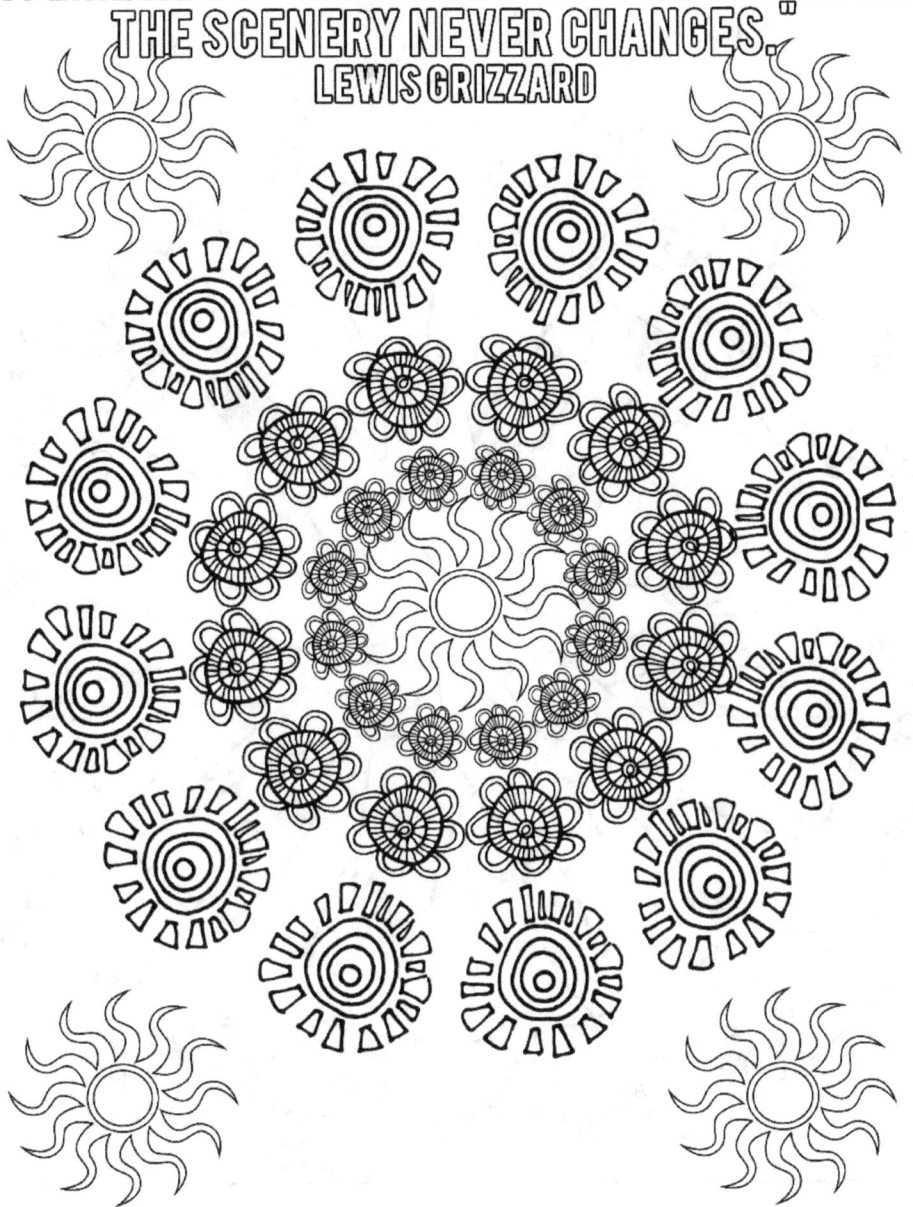

"SPECTACULAR ACHIEVEMENT IS ALWAYS PRECEDED BY
UNSPECTACULAR PREPARATION."
ROBERT H. SCHULLER

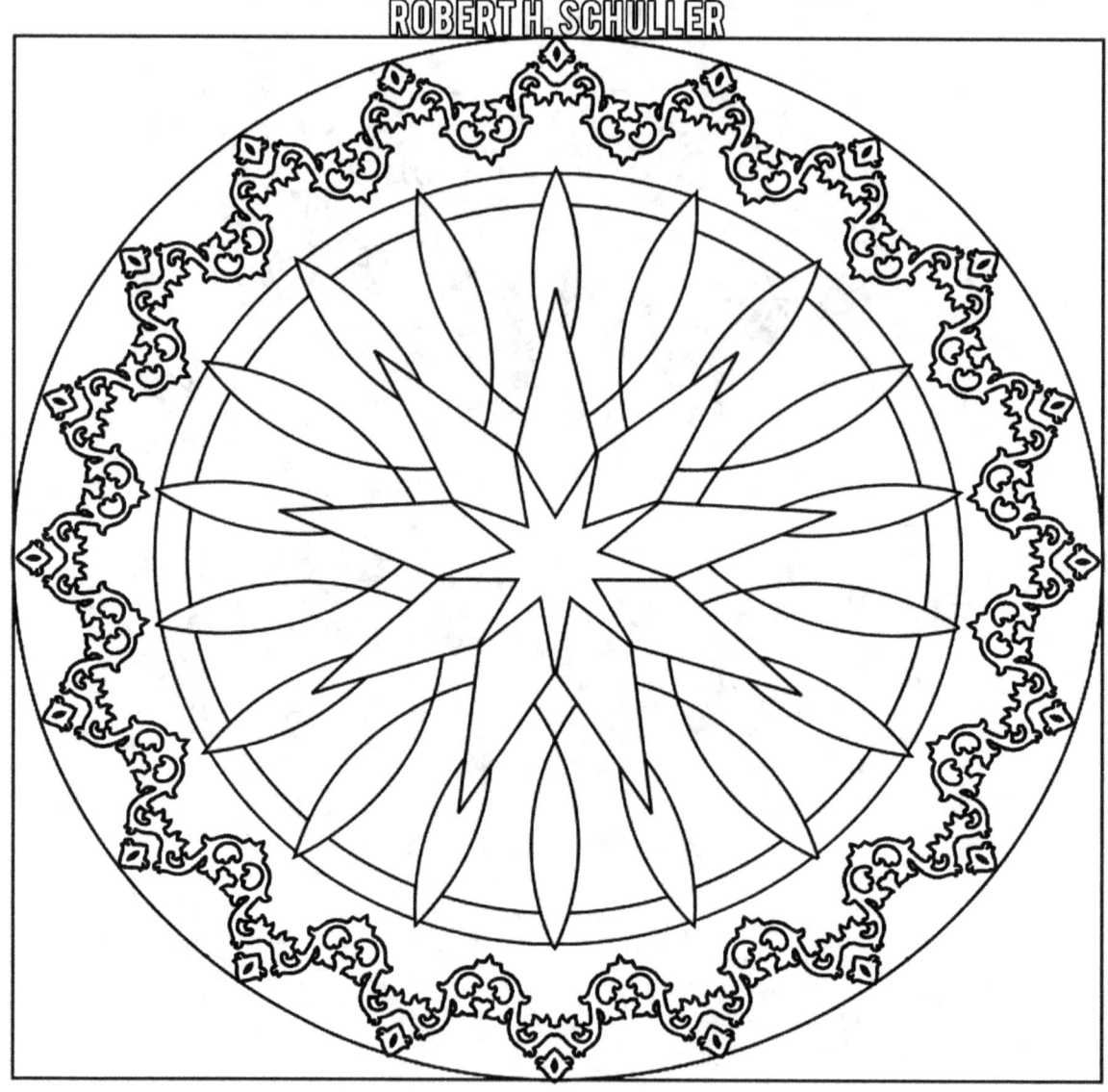

"A GOAL PROPERLY SET IS HALFWAY REACHED."
ABRAHAM LINCOLN

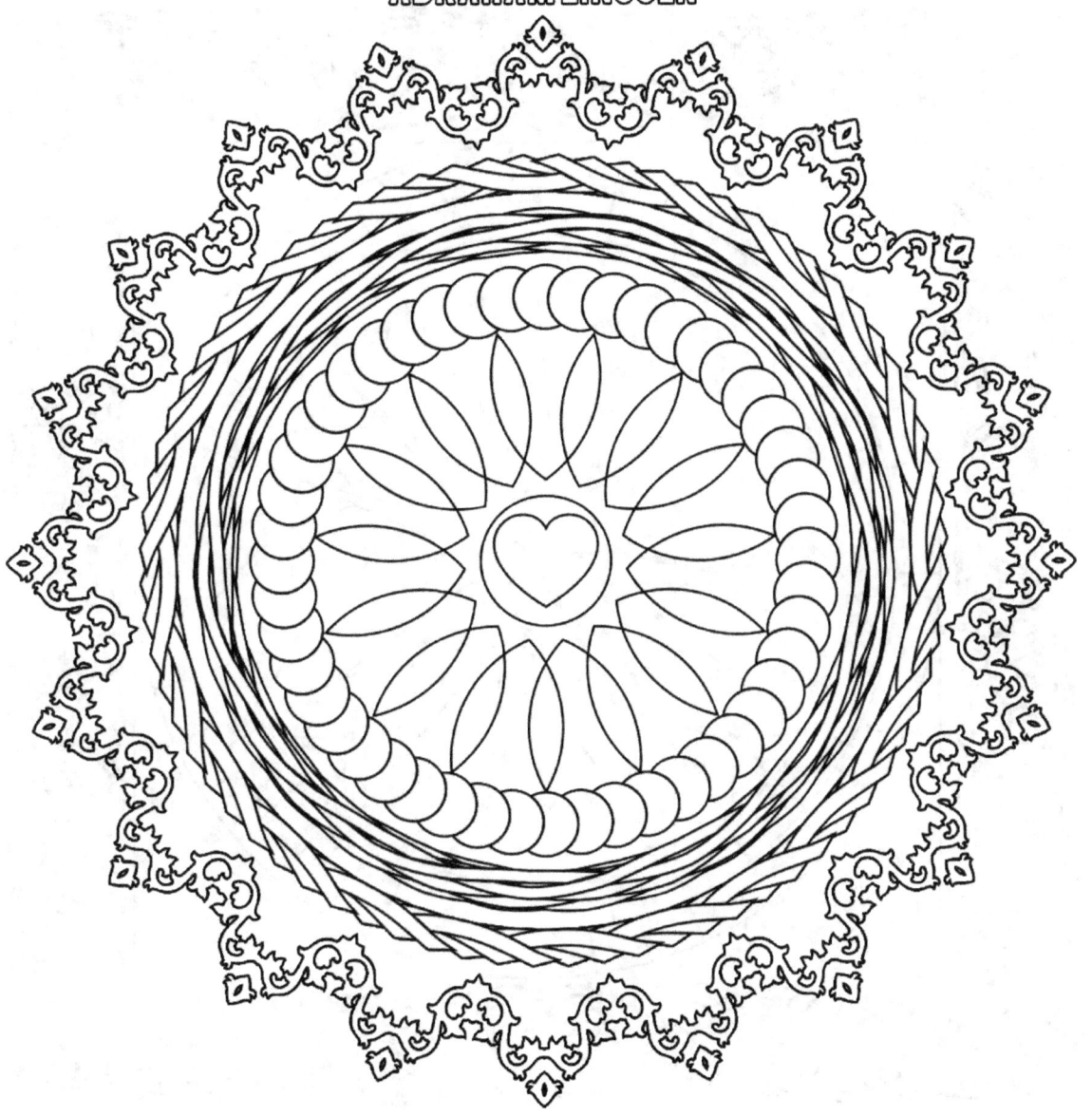

"AN AIM IN LIFE IS THE ONLY FORTUNE WORTH FINDING."
ROBERT LOUIS STEVENSON

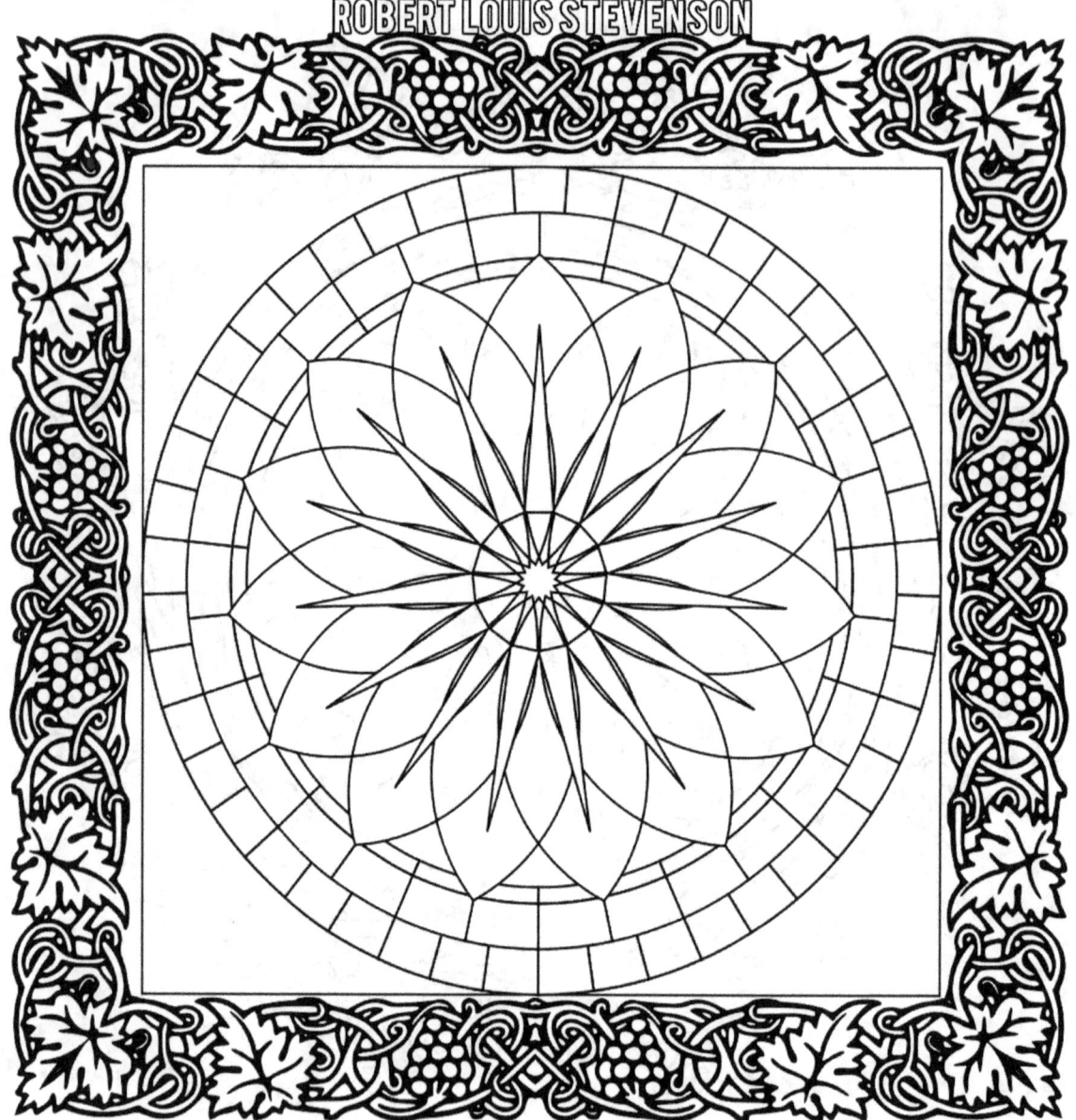

"THERE IS MORE TO LIFE THAN INCREASING ITS SPEED."
MAHATMA GANDHI

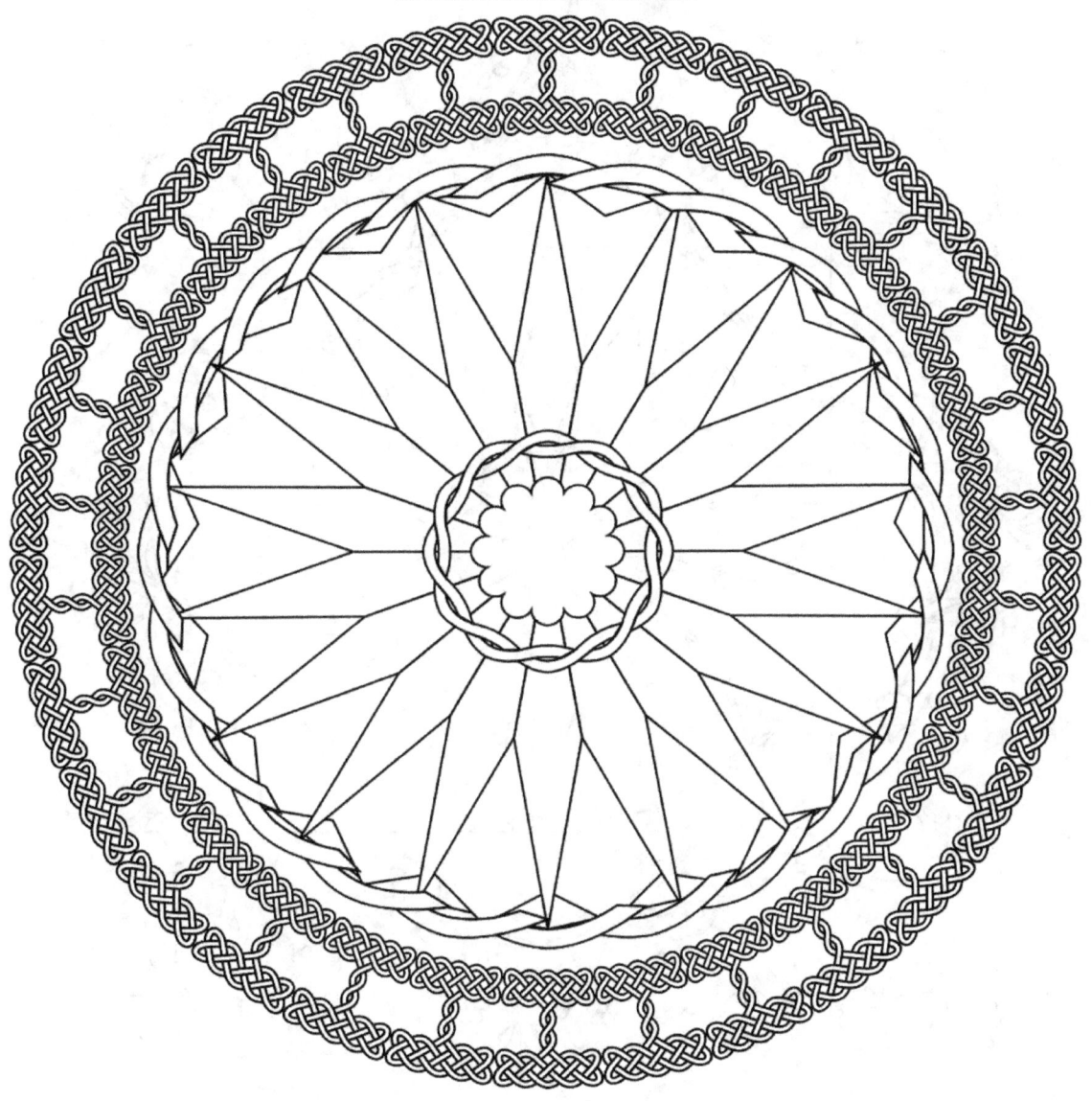

"BEGIN, BE BOLD AND VENTURE TO BE WISE."
HORACE

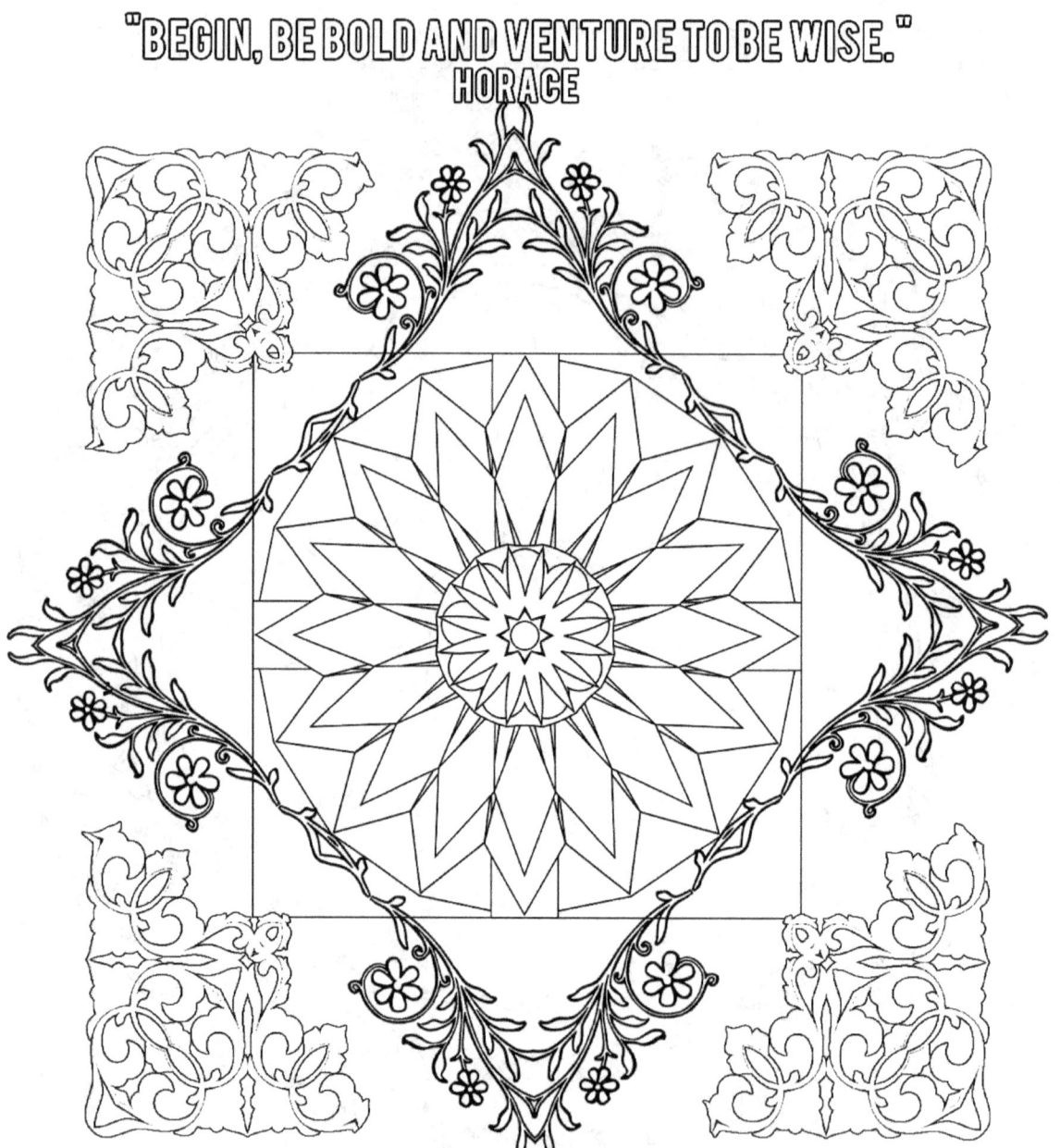

"COMMON SENSE IS THE KNACK OF SEEING THINGS
AS THEY ARE,
AND DOING THINGS AS THEY OUGHT TO BE DONE."
HARRIET BEECHER STOWE

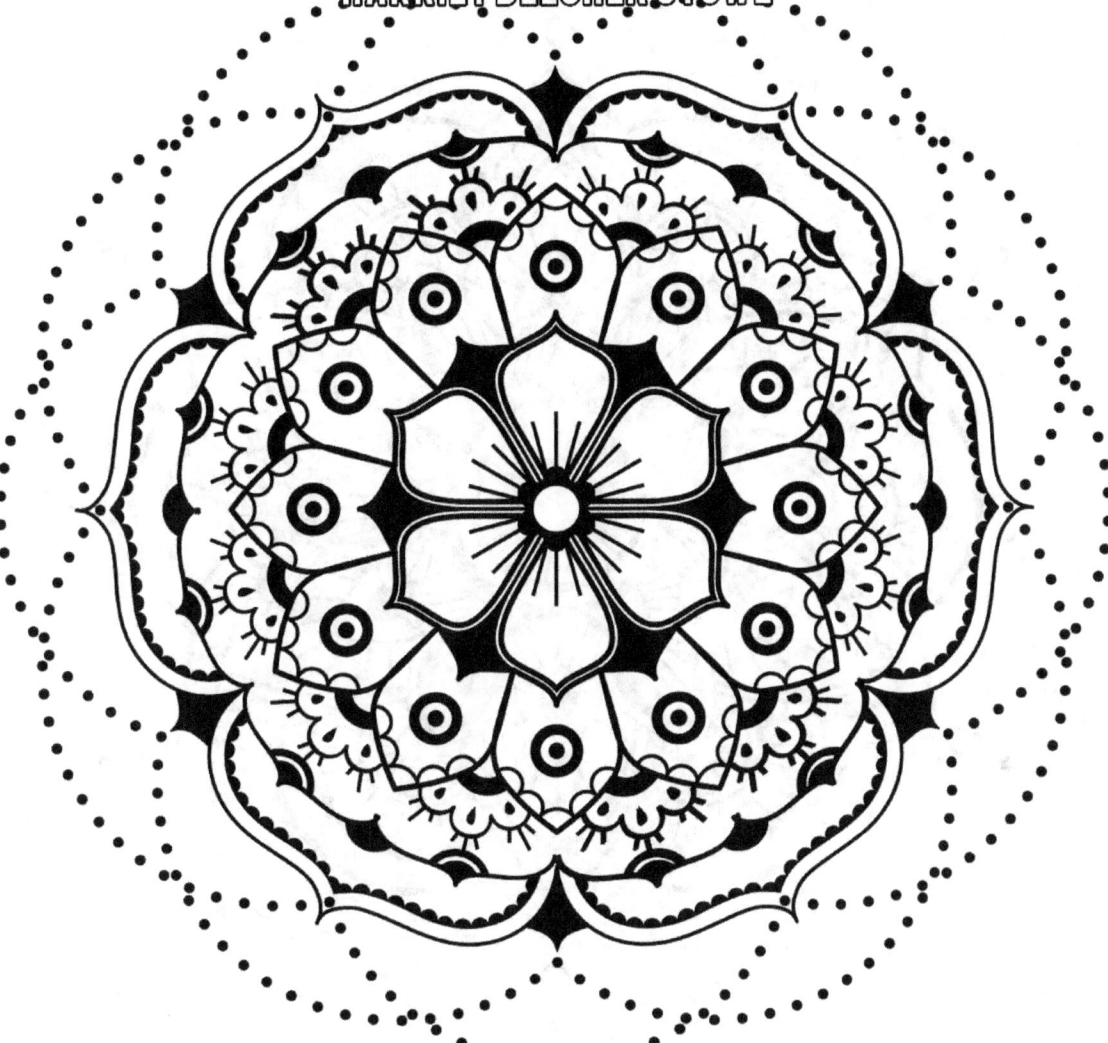

"THE WHOLE SECRET OF LIFE
IS TO BE INTERESTED IN ONE THING PROFOUNDLY
AND IN A THOUSAND THINGS WELL."
HUGH WALPOLE

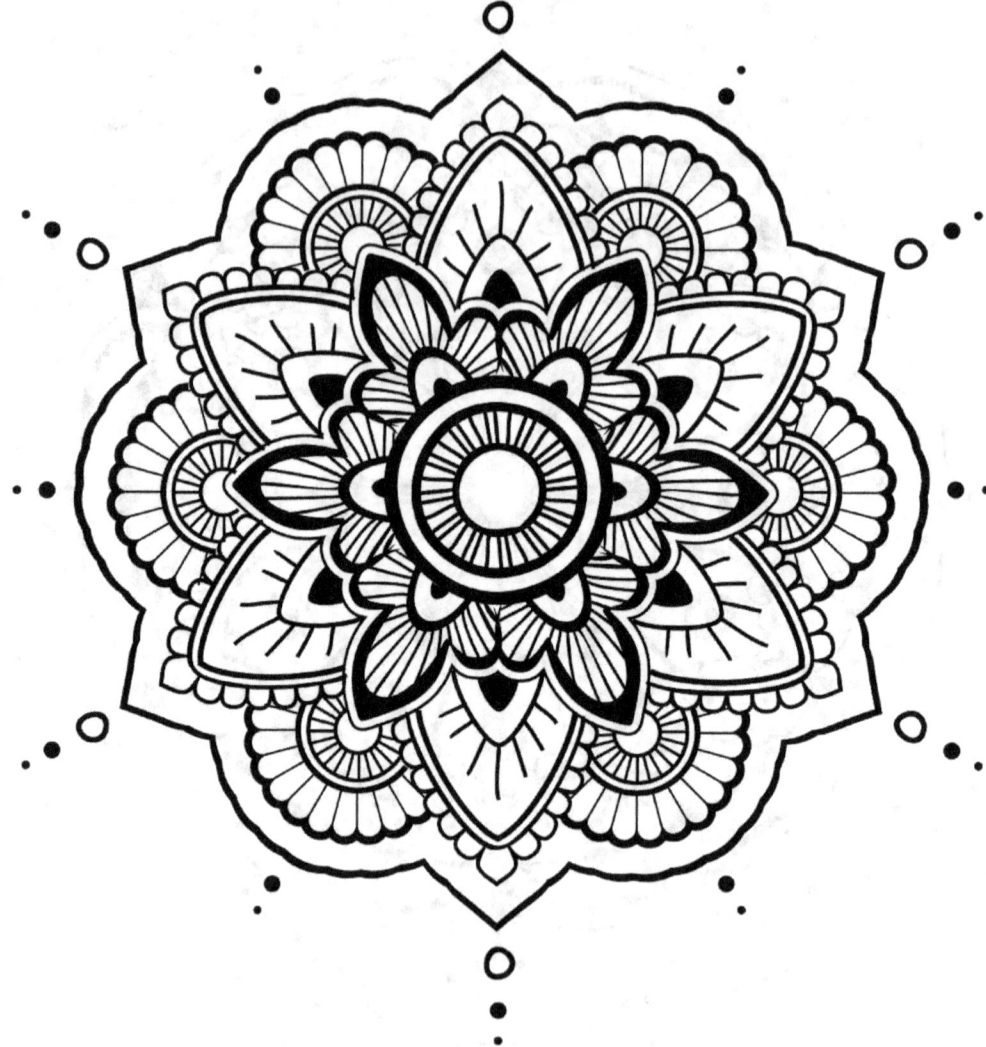

"EACH DAY OF OUR LIVES WE MAKE DEPOSITS
IN THE MEMORY BANKS OF OUR CHILDREN."
CHARLES R. SWINDOLL

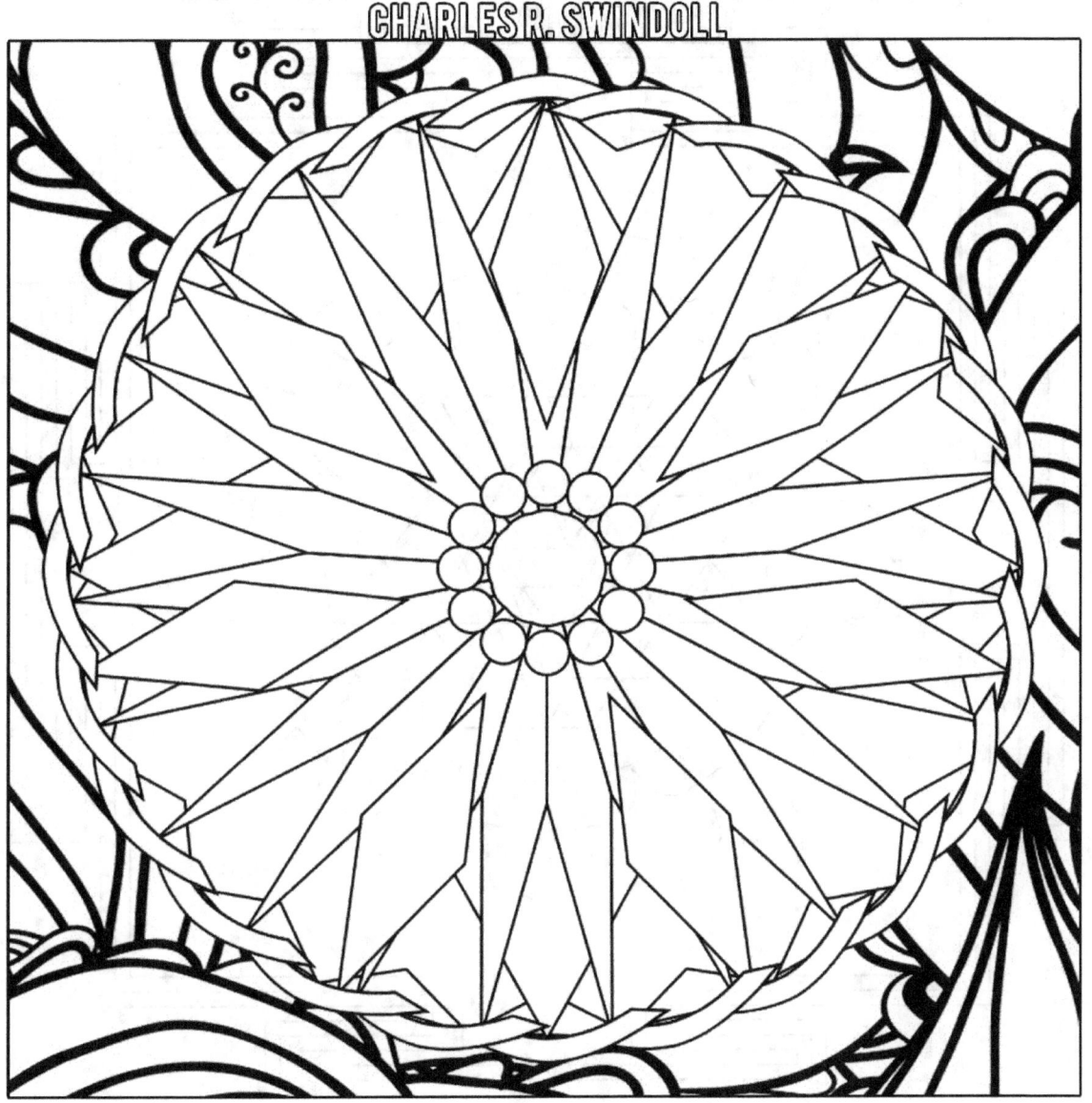

"TOO MANY PEOPLE DON'T CARE WHAT HAPPENS
SO LONG AS IT DOESN'T HAPPEN TO THEM."
WILLIAM HOWARD TAFT

"FAR BETTER IT IS TO DARE MIGHTY THINGS,
TO WIN GLORIOUS TRIUMPHS,
EVEN THOUGH CHECKERED BY FAILURE,
THAN TO TAKE RANK WITH THOSE POOR SPIRITS
WHO NEITHER ENJOY MUCH NOR SUFFER MUCH,
BECAUSE THEY LIVE IN THE GRAY TWILIGHT
THAT KNOWS NOT VICTORY NOR DEFEAT."
THEODORE ROOSEVELT

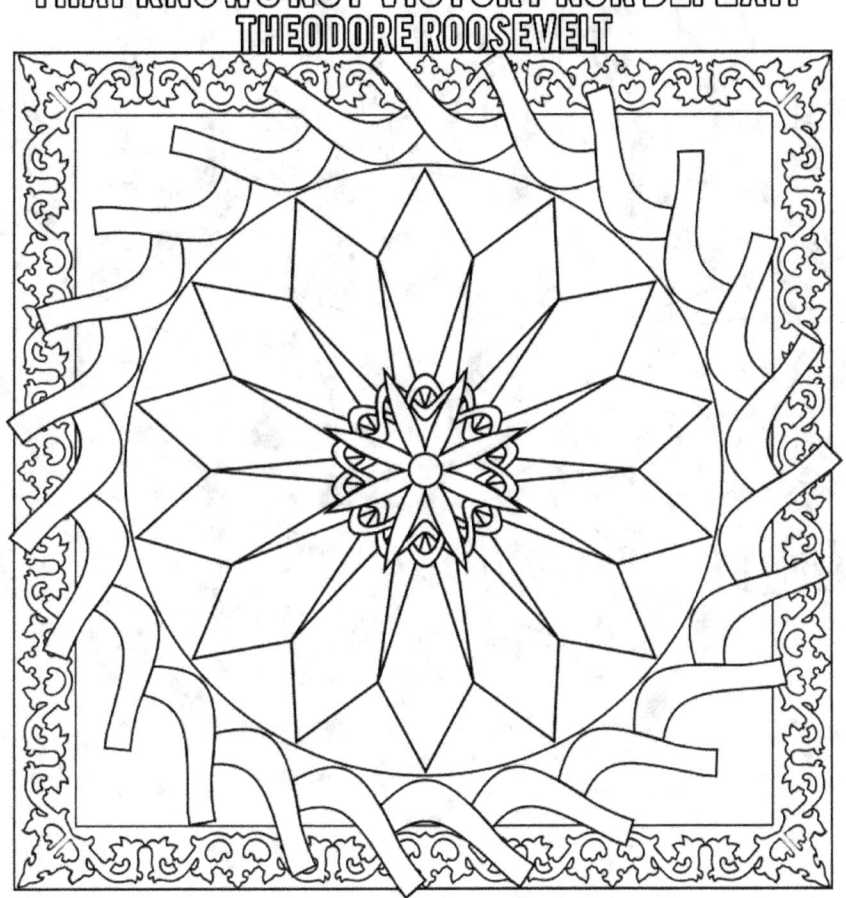

"VISION WITHOUT ACTION IS A DAYDREAM,
ACTION WITHOUT VISION IS A NIGHTMARE."
JAPANESE PROVERB

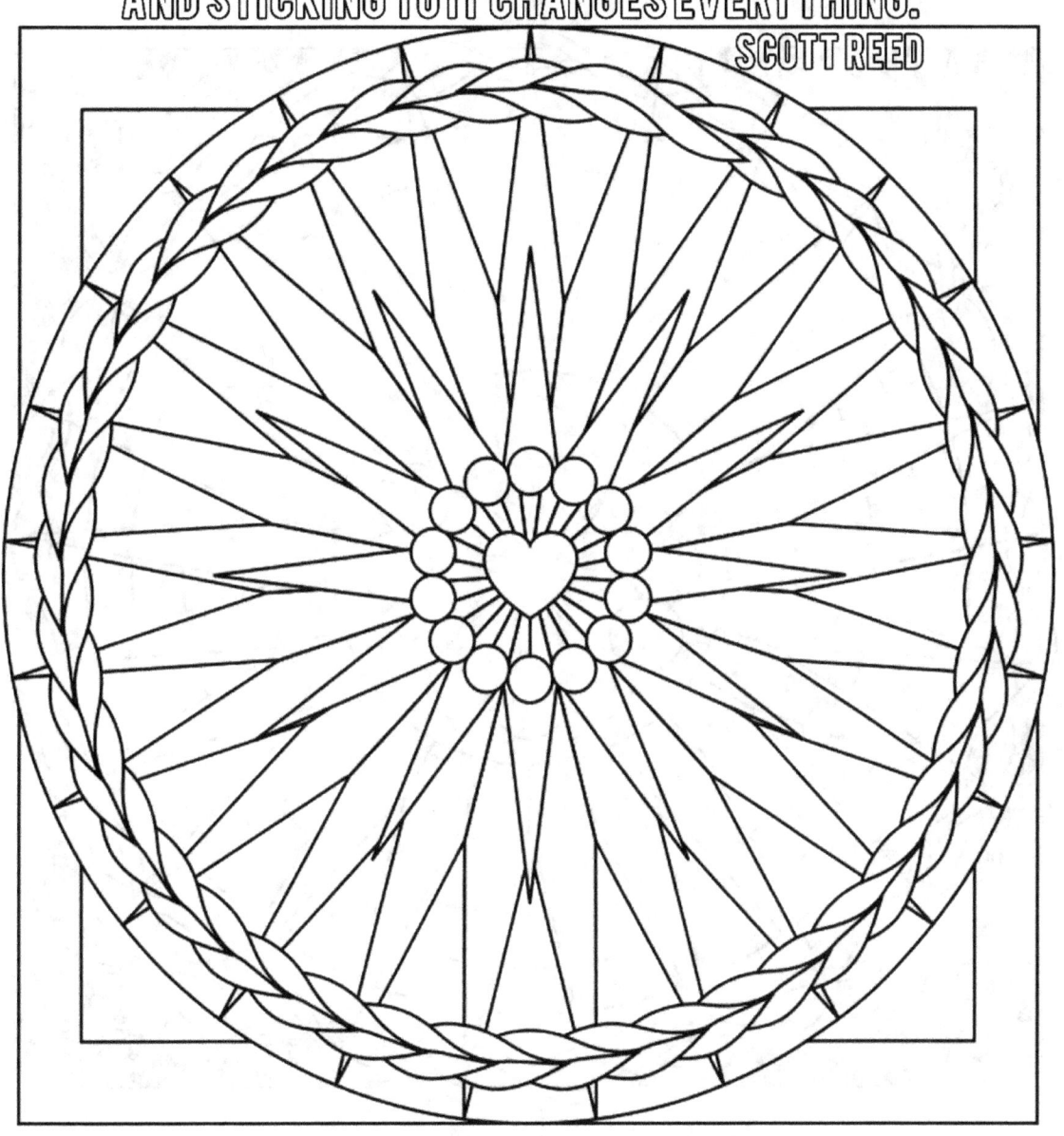

"THIS ONE STEP, CHOOSING A GOAL
AND STICKING TO IT CHANGES EVERYTHING."
SCOTT REED

"BEGIN, BE BOLD AND VENTURE TO BE WISE."
HORACE

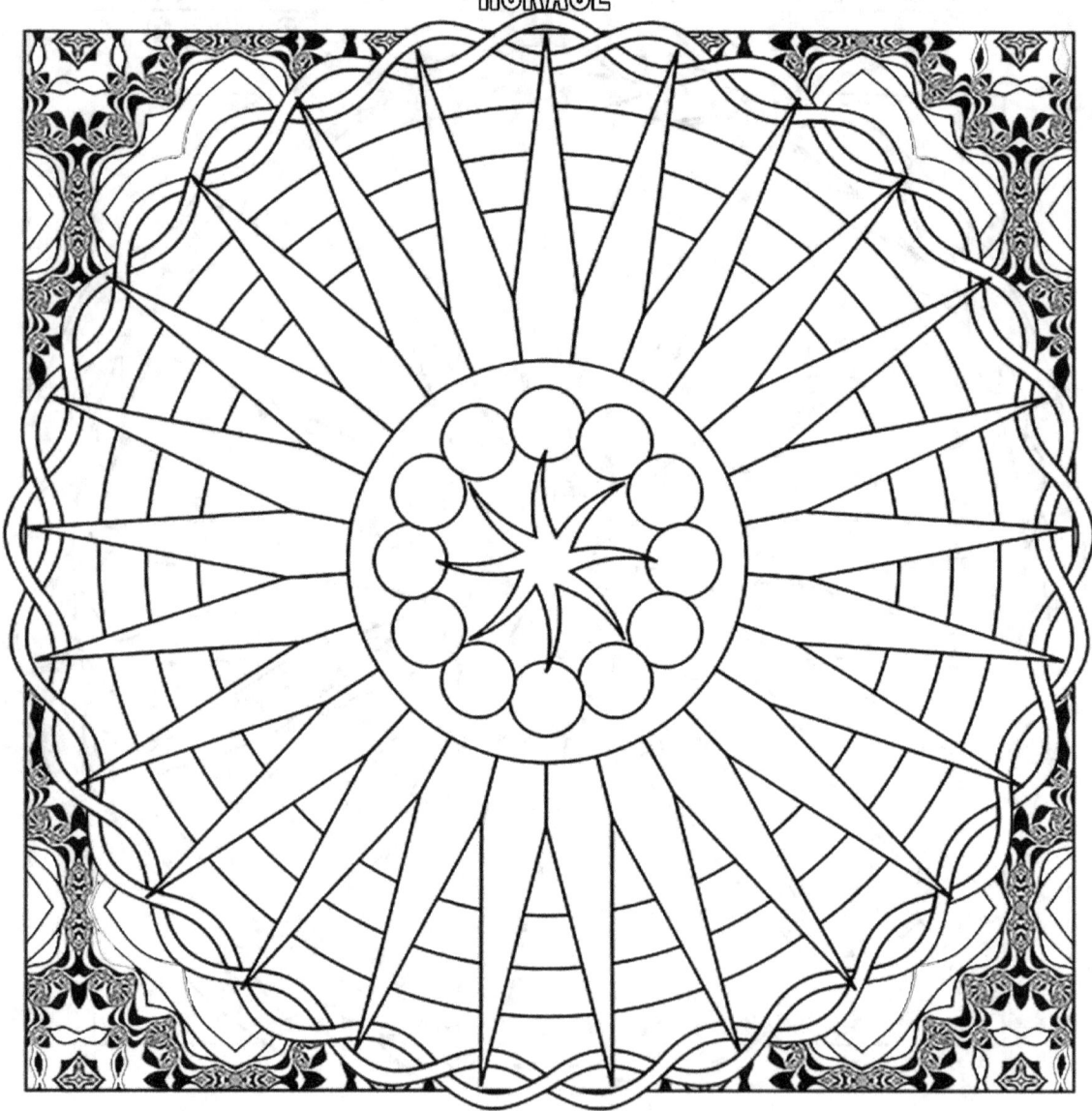

"DO WHAT YOU CAN,
WITH WHAT YOU HAVE, WHERE YOU ARE."
THEODORE ROOSEVELT

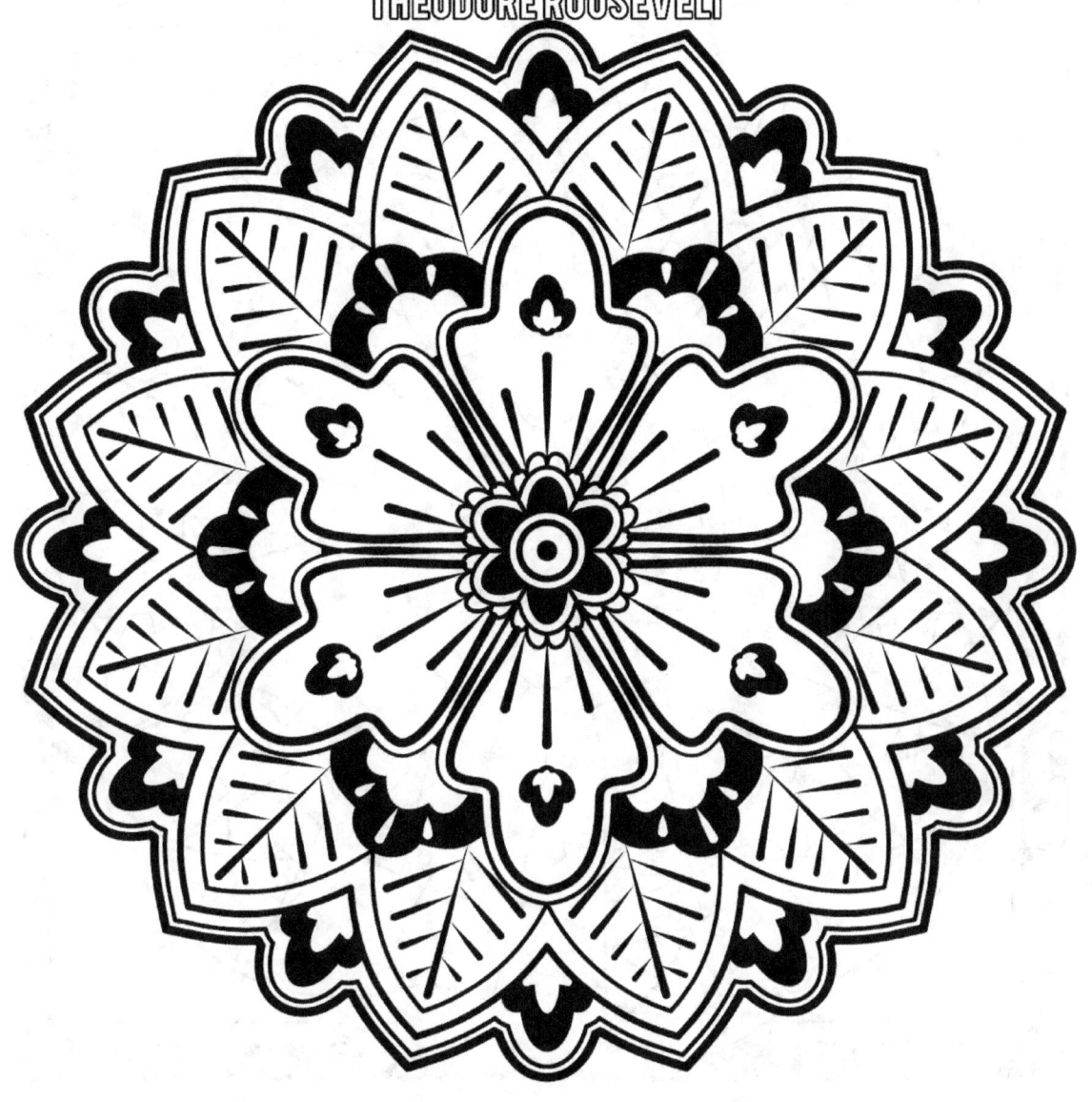

"AS IS OUR CONFIDENCE, SO IS OUR CAPACITY."
WILLIAM HAZLITT

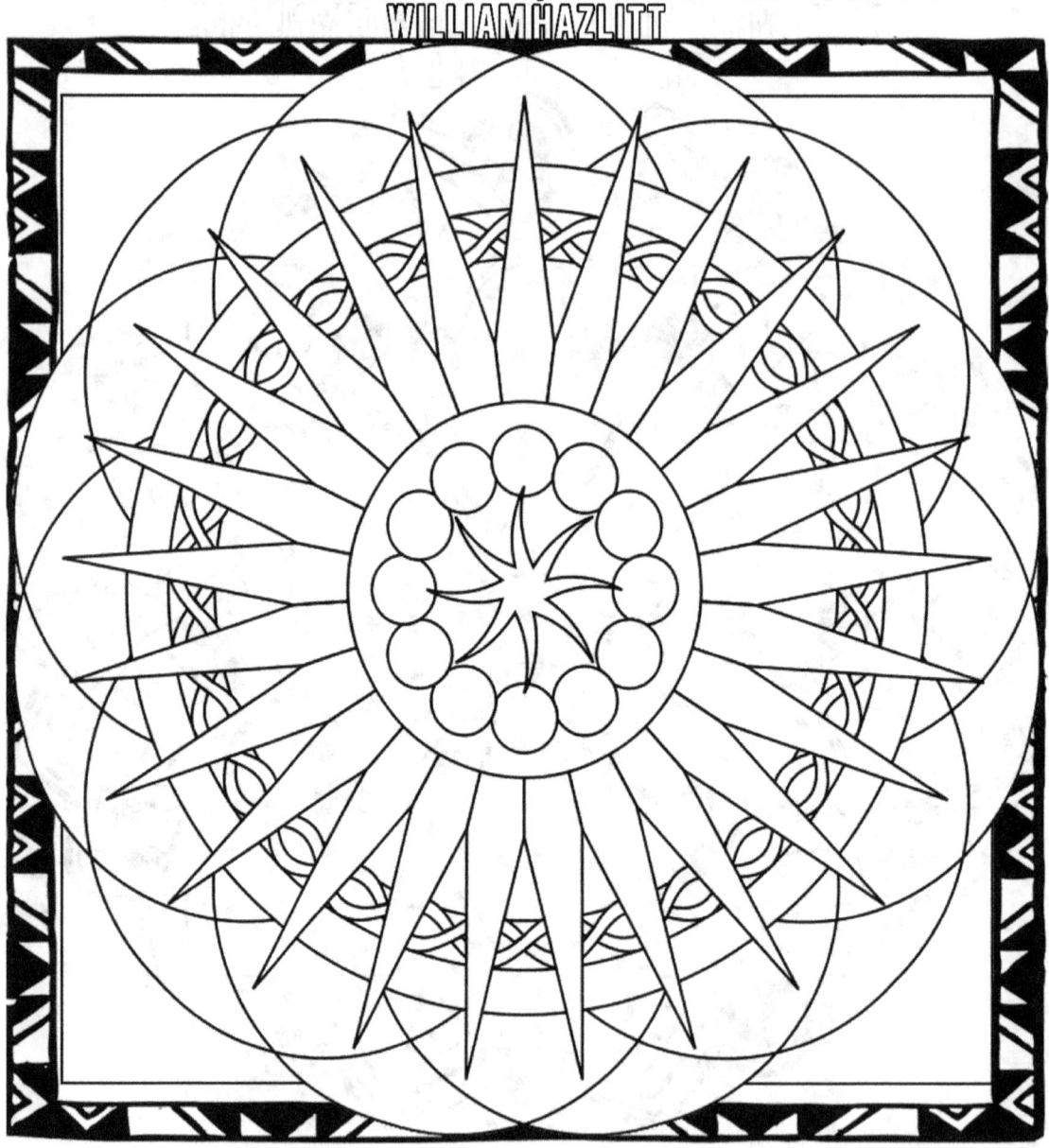

"GREAT MINDS HAVE PURPOSES, OTHERS HAVE WISHES."
WASHINGTON IRVING

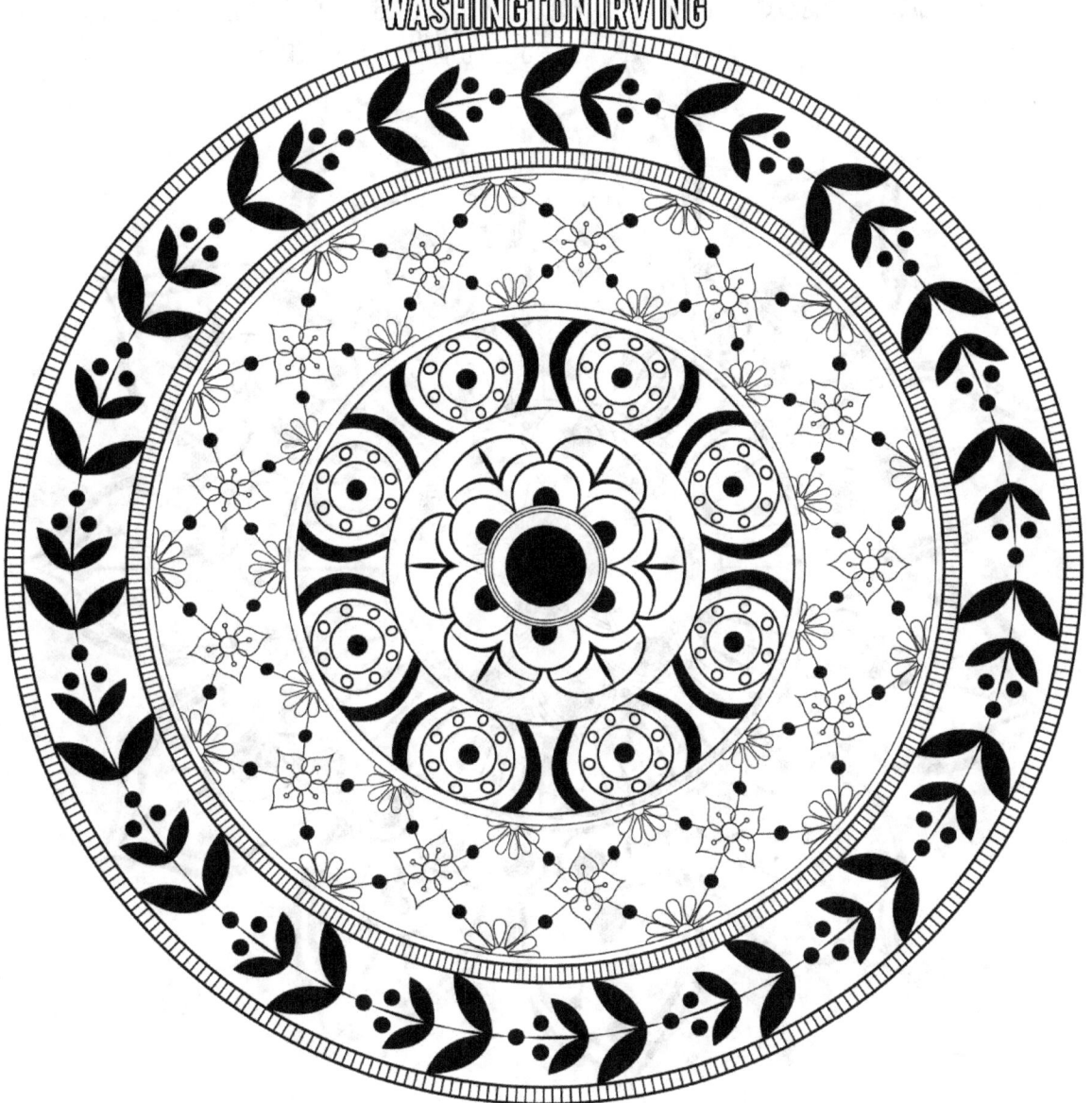

"IN MATTER OF PRINCIPLE, STAND LIKE A ROCK;
IN MATTERS OF TASTE, SWIM WITH THE CURRENT."
THOMAS JEFFERSON

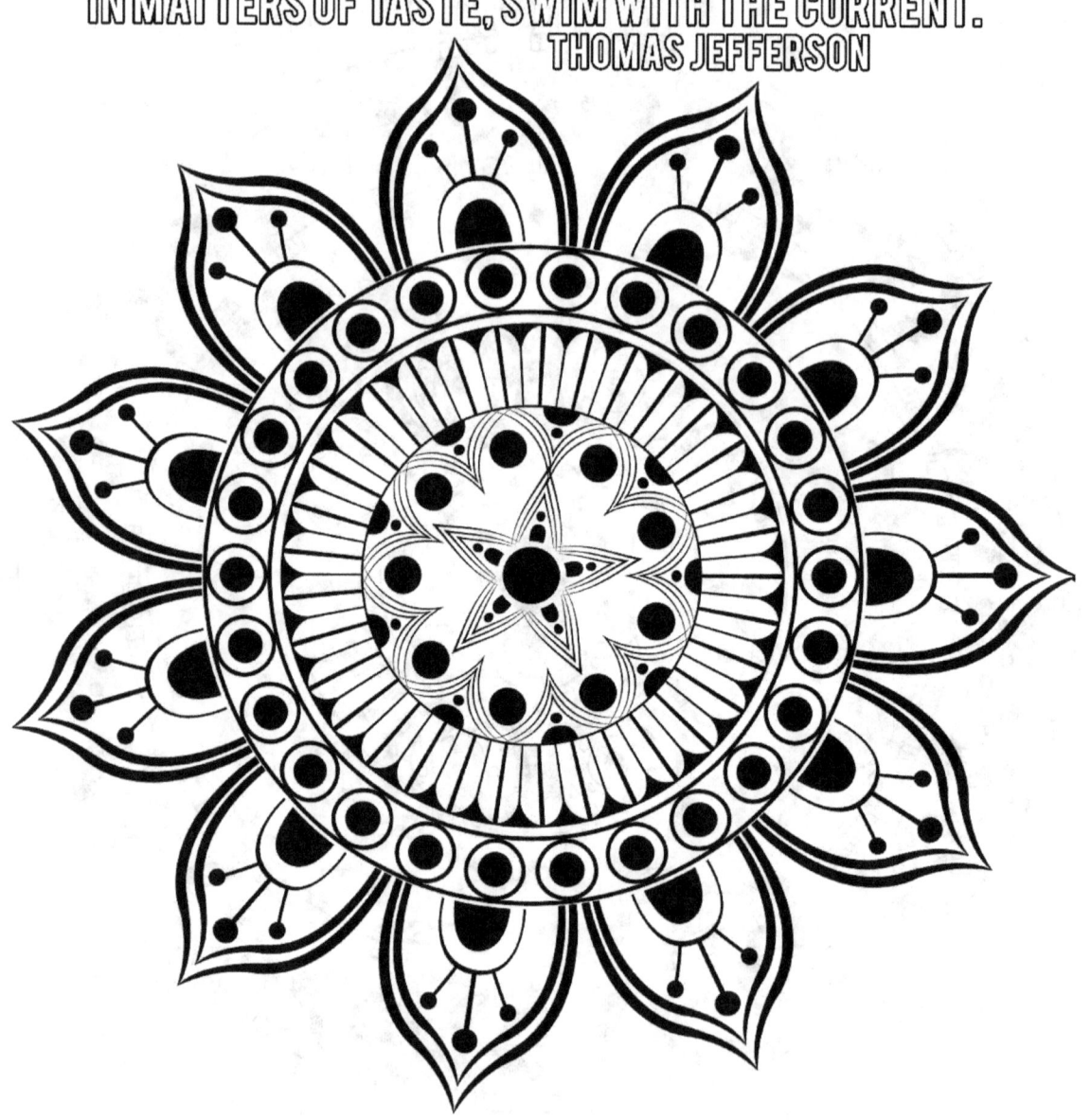

"DON'T DWELL ON REALITY;
IT WILL ONLY KEEP YOU FROM GREATNESS."
REV. RANDALL R. MCBRIDE, JR.

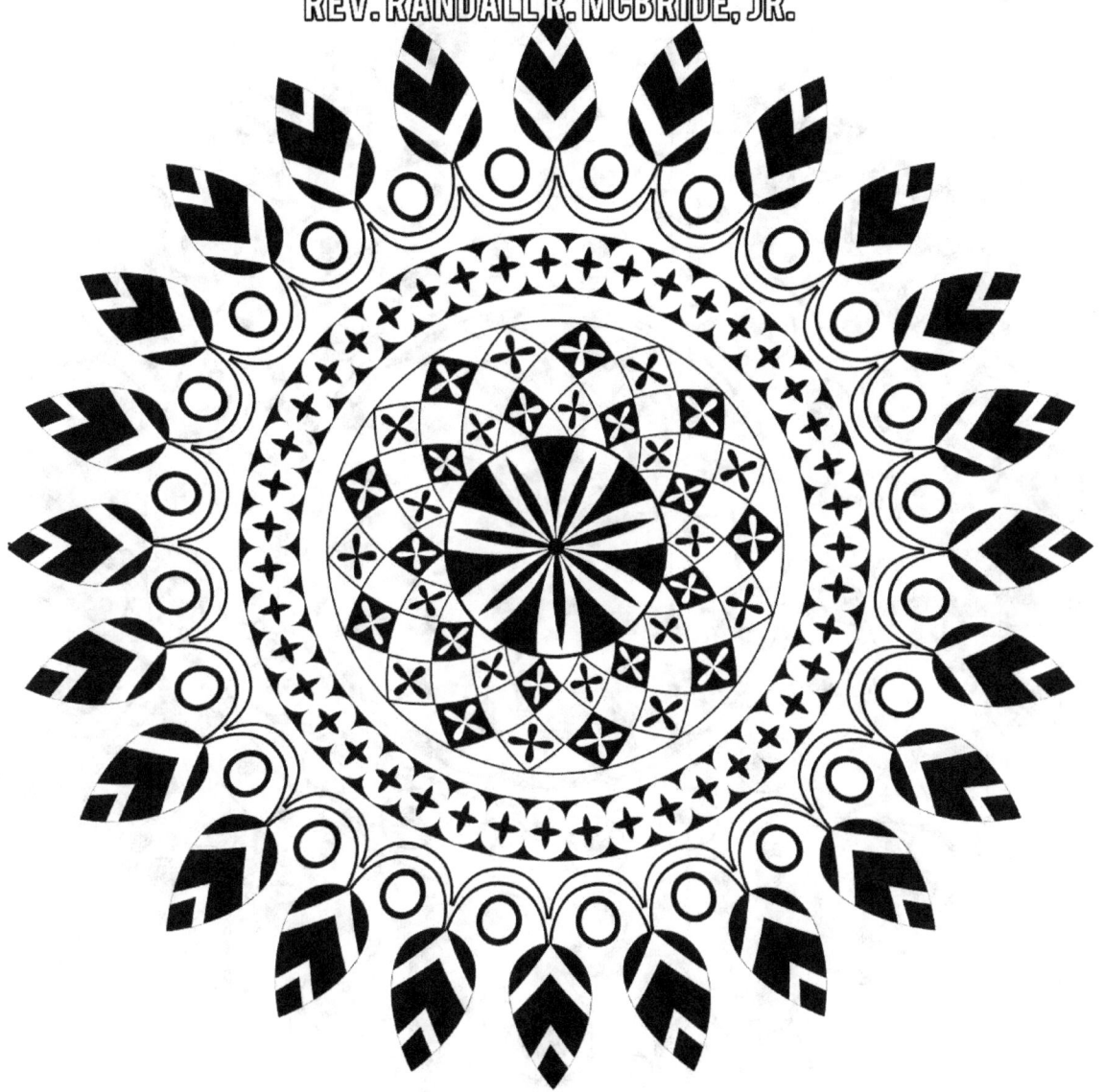

"HOW SOON 'NOT NOW' BECOMES 'NEVER.'"
MARTIN LUTHER

"WHAT WE SEE DEPENDS MAINLY ON WHAT WE LOOK FOR."
JOHN LUBBOCK

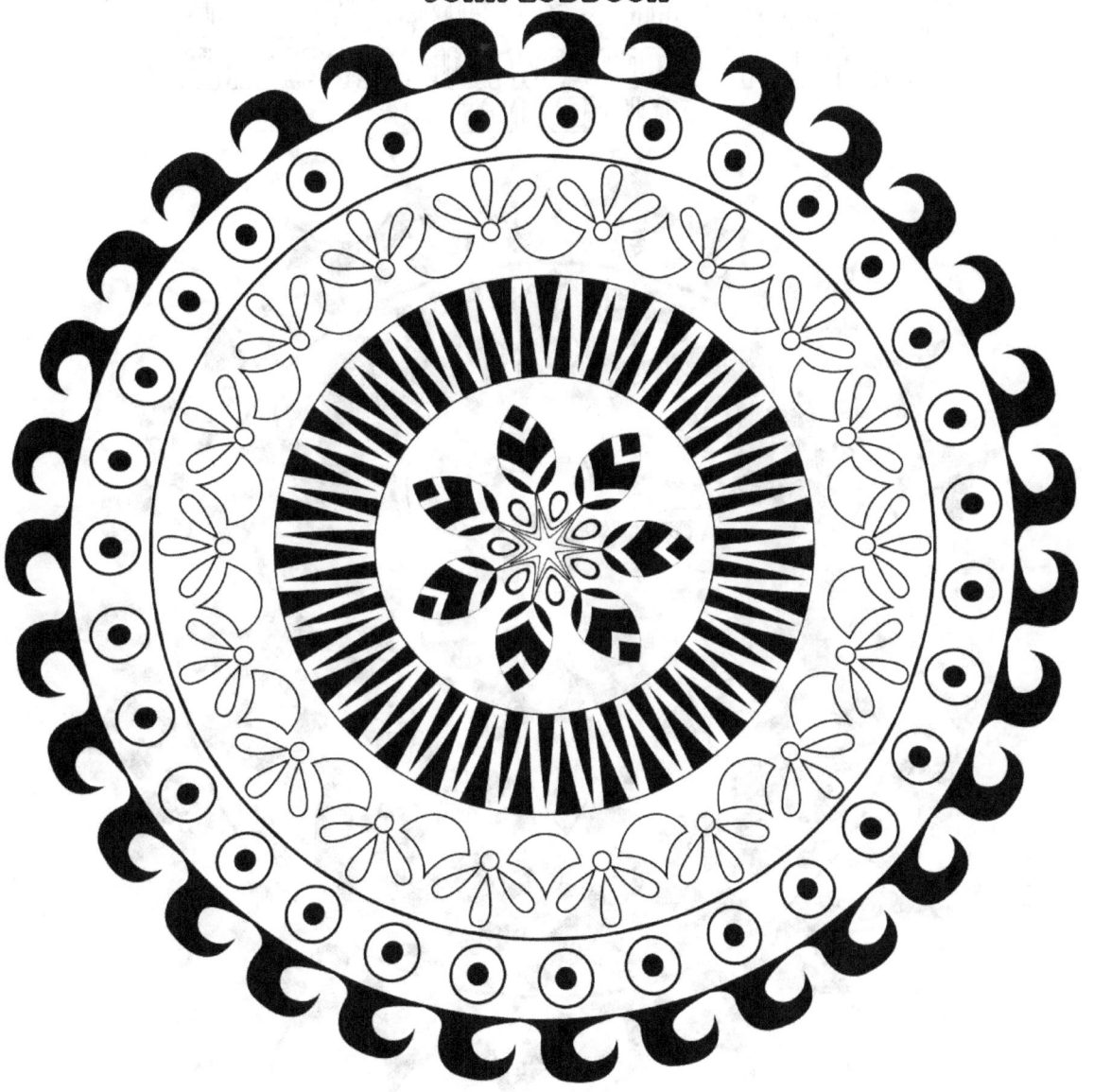

"THE GREATEST DANGER FOR MOST OF US
IS NOT THAT OUR AIM IS TOO HIGH AND WE MISS IT,
BUT THAT IT IS TOO LOW AND WE REACH IT."
MICHELANGELO

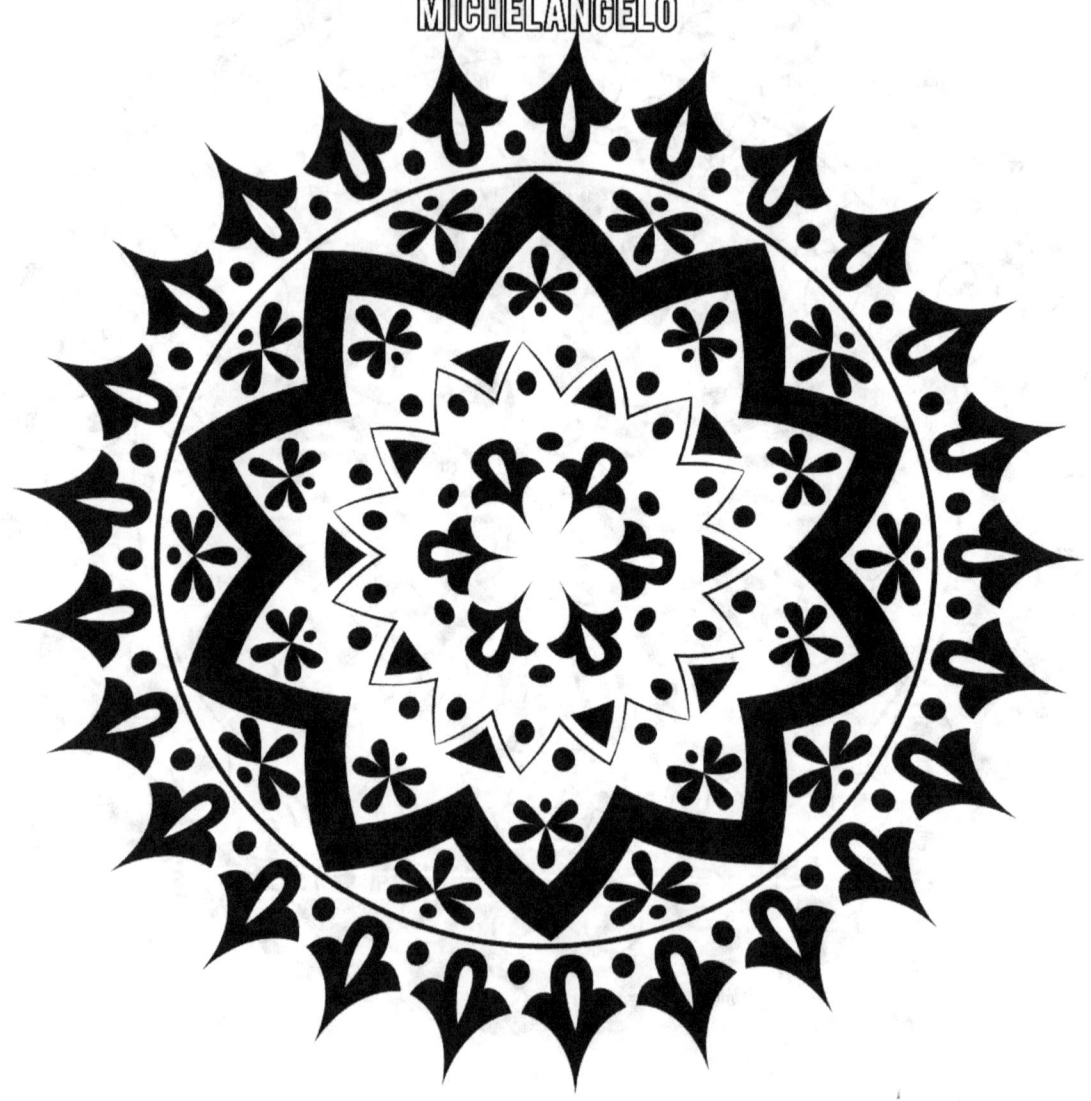

"THE WHOLE LIFE OF MAN IS BUT A POINT OF TIME;
LET US ENJOY IT."
PLUTARCH

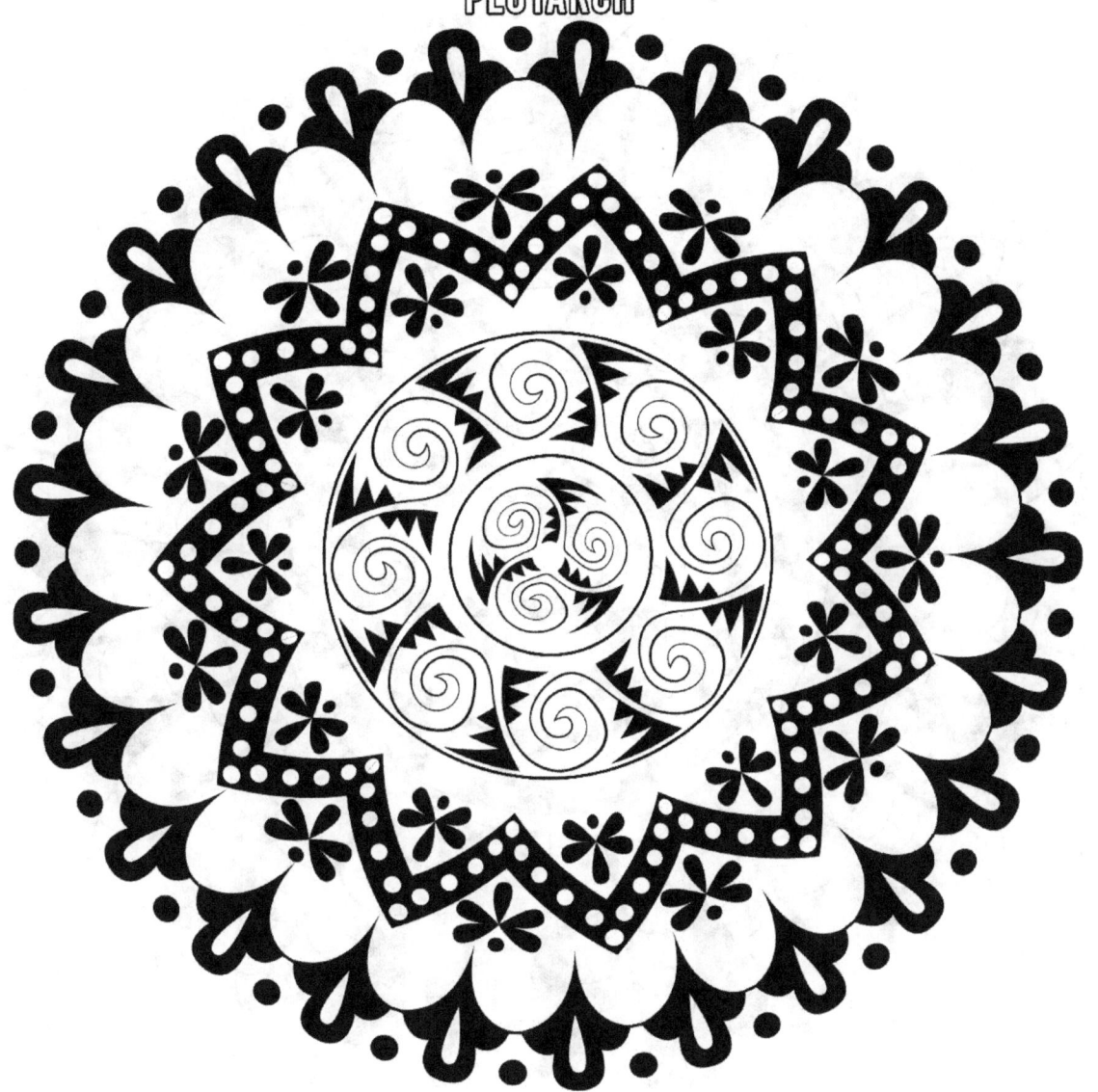

"THE QUESTION ISN'T WHO IS GOING TO LET ME;
IT'S WHO IS GOING TO STOP ME."
AYN RAND

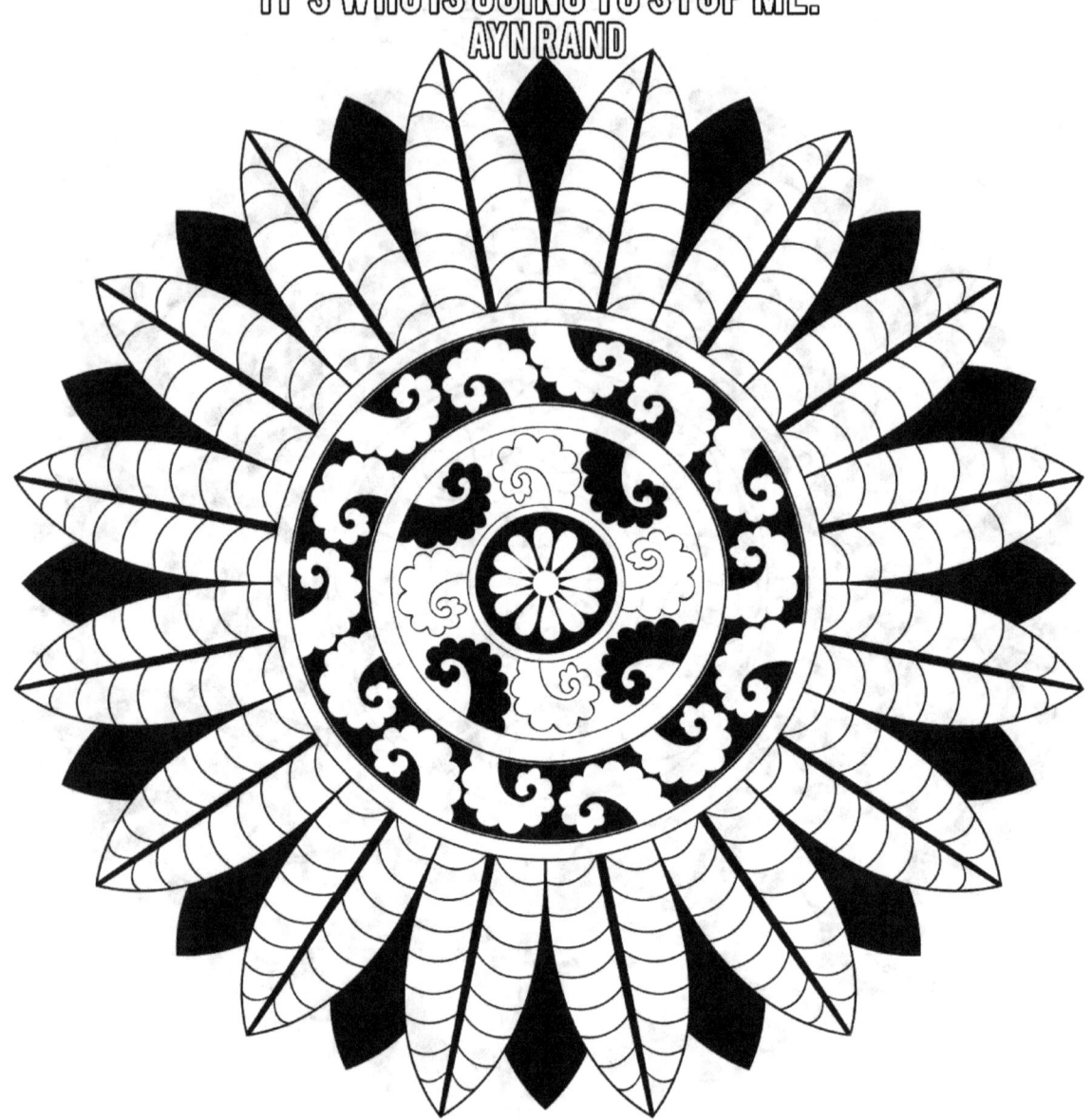

"THE TRAGEDY OF LIFE IS NOT THAT IT ENDS SO SOON,
BUT THAT WE WAIT SO LONG TO BEGIN IT."
W. M. LEWIS

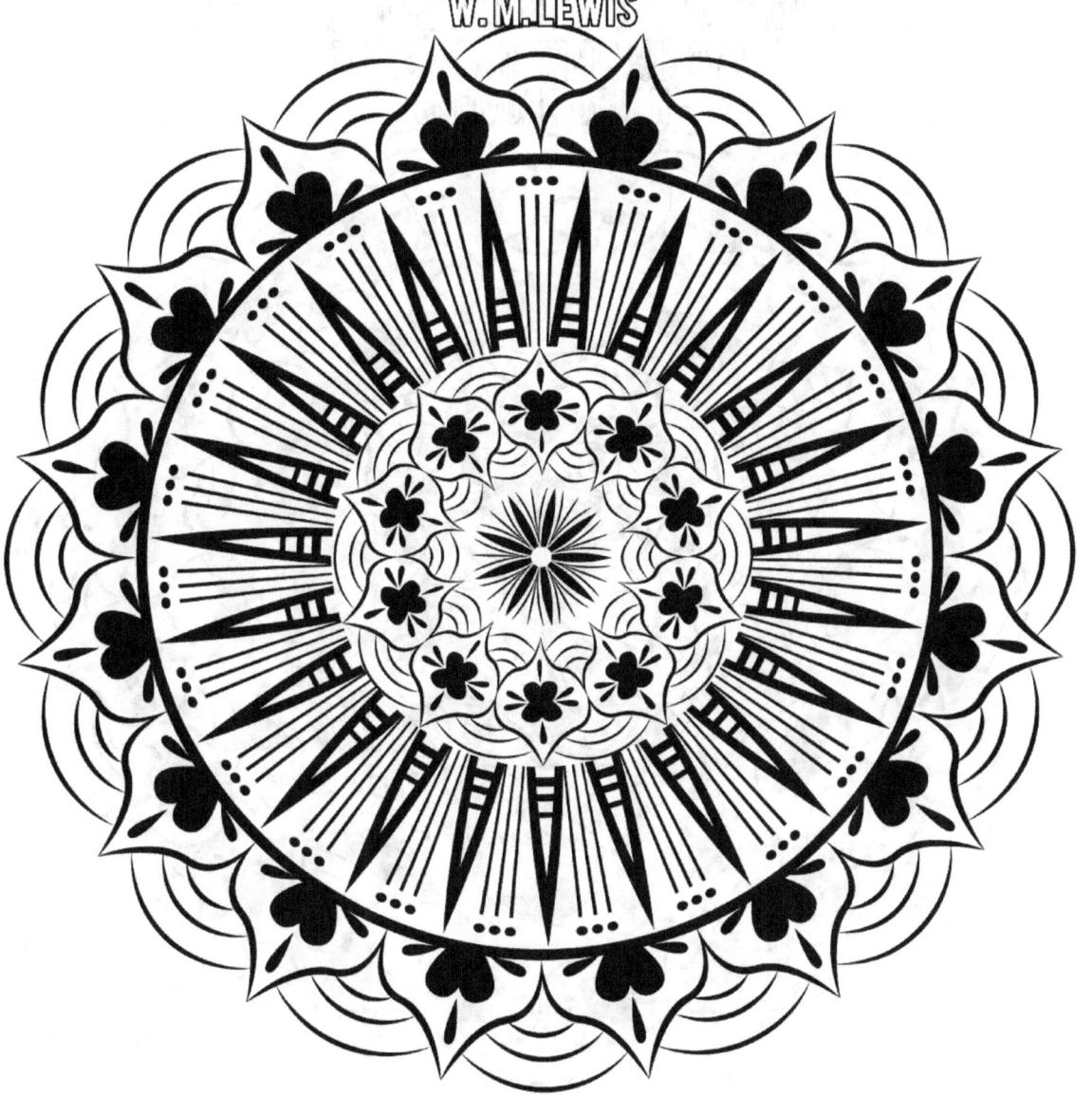

"THERE IS NOTHING NOBLE ABOUT BEING SUPERIOR
TO SOME OTHER MAN.
THE TRUE NOBILITY IS IN BEING SUPERIOR
TO YOUR PREVIOUS SELF."
HINDU PROVERB

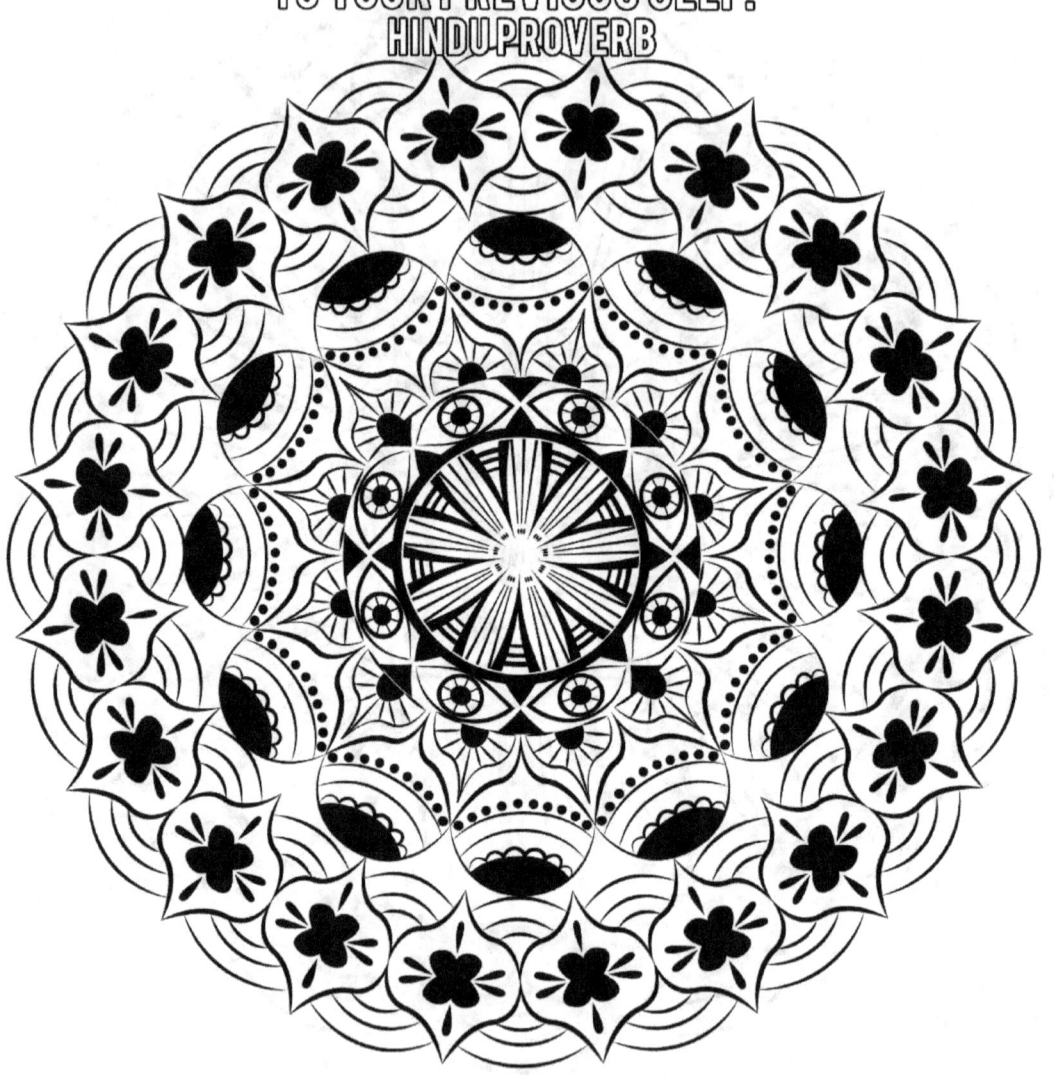

"PATIENCE, PERSISTENCE AND PERSPIRATION
MAKE AN UNBEATABLE COMBINATION FOR SUCCESS."
NAPOLEAN HILL

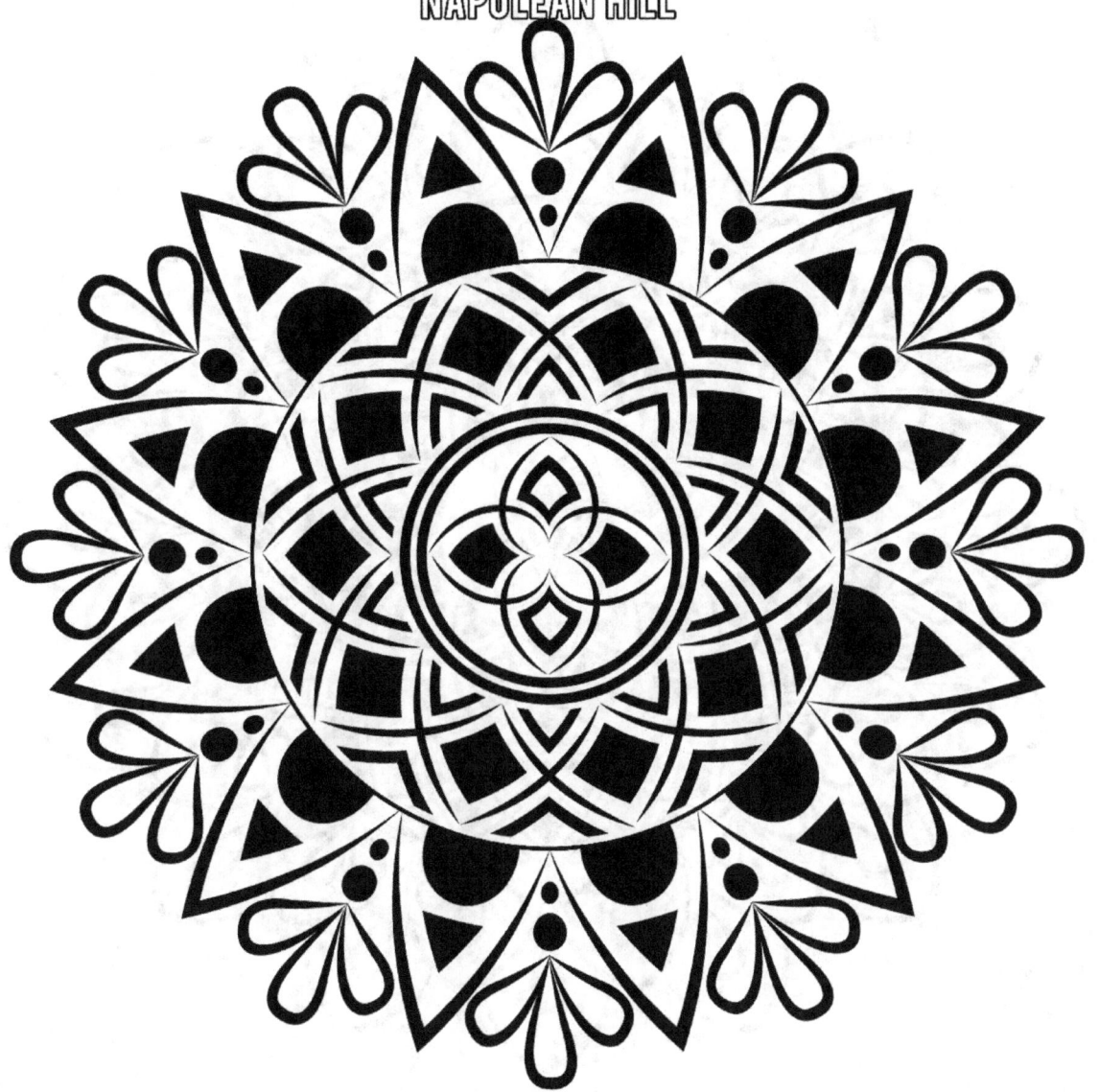

"THE BRIGHTER YOU ARE, THE MORE YOU HAVE TO LEARN."
DON HEROLD

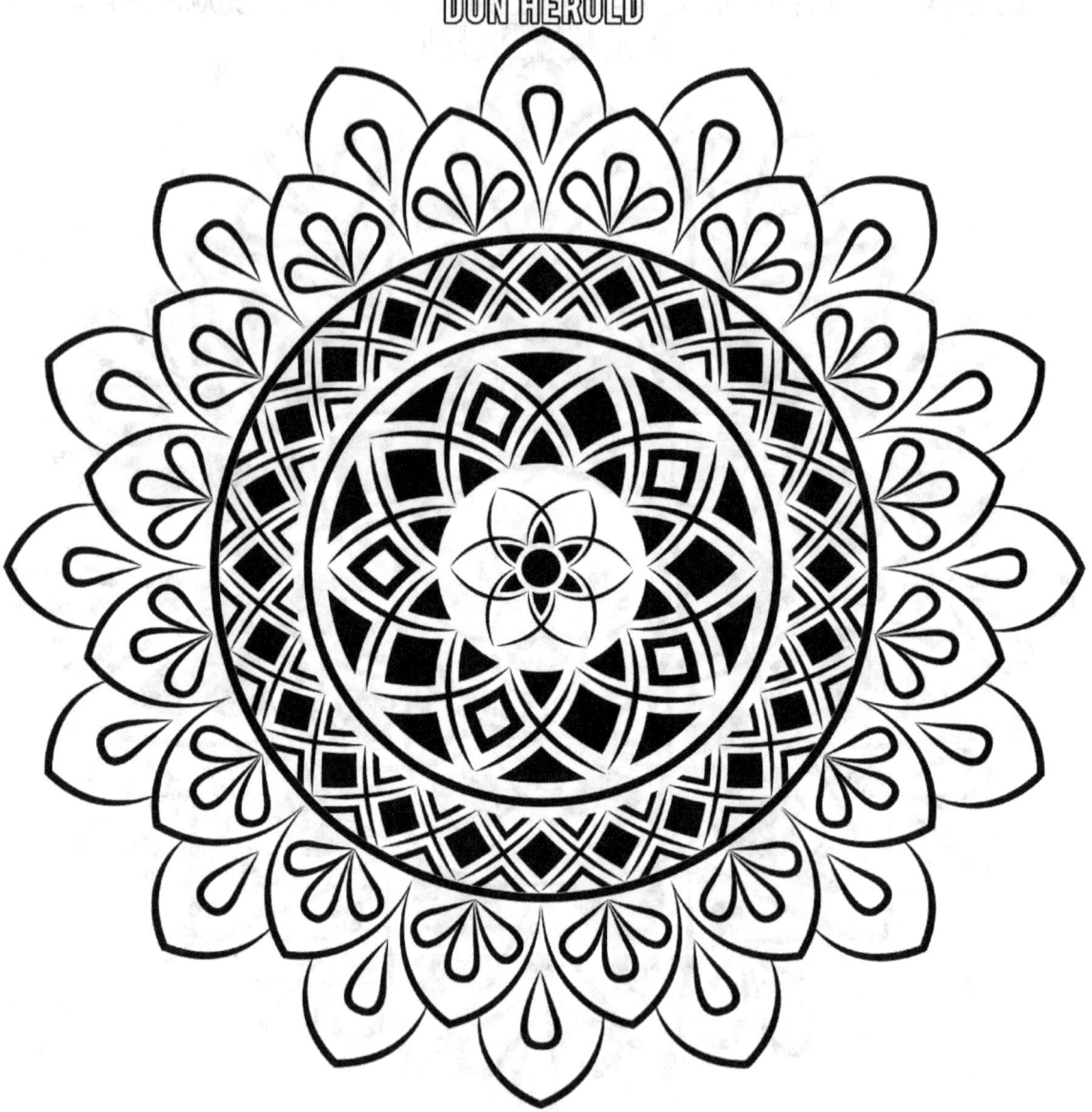

"CONSTANT DRIPPING HOLLOWS OUT A STONE."
LUCRETIUS

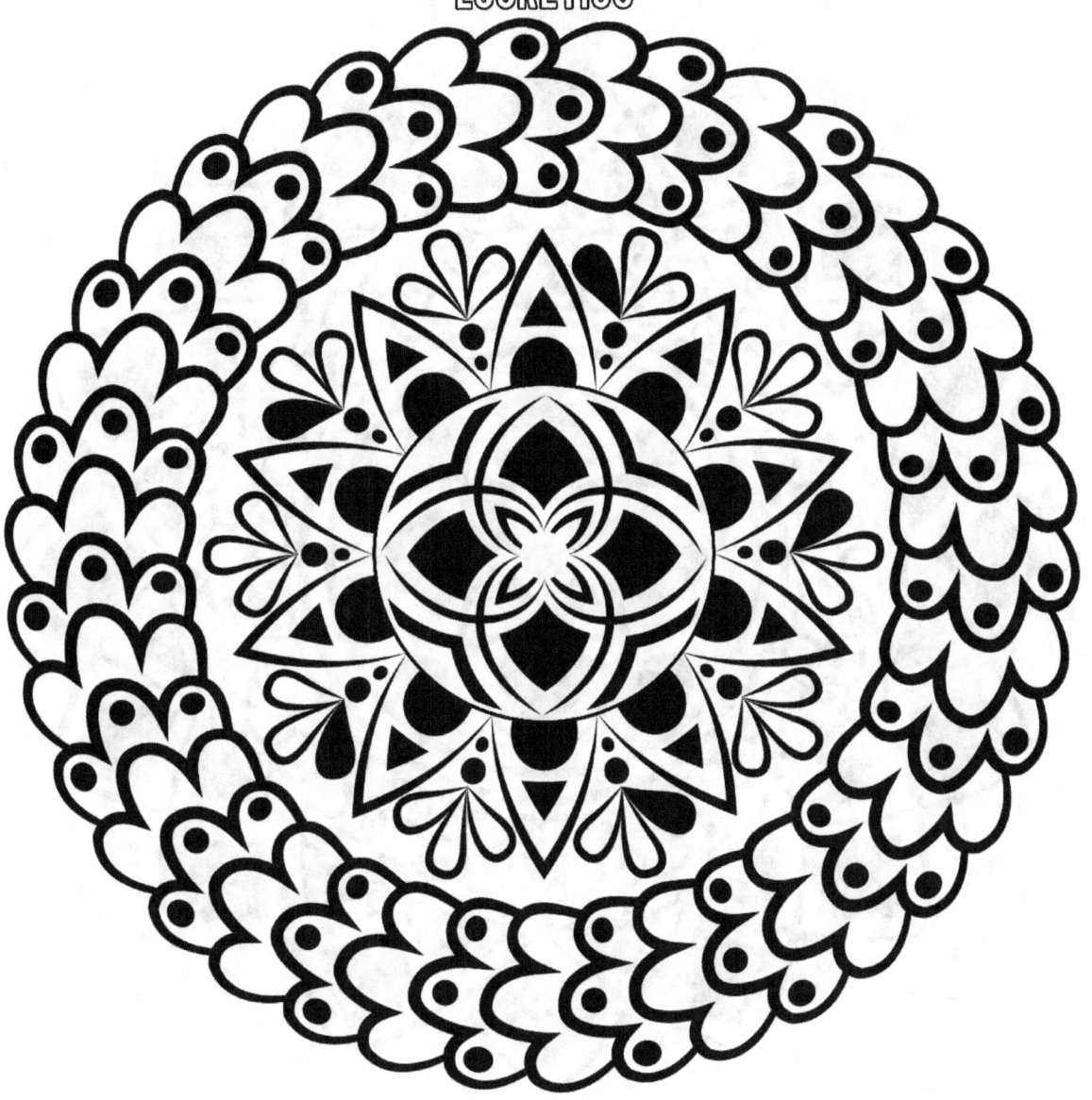

"IF ONE DOES NOT KNOW TO WHICH PORT ONE IS SAILING, NO WIND IS FAVORABLE."
SENECA

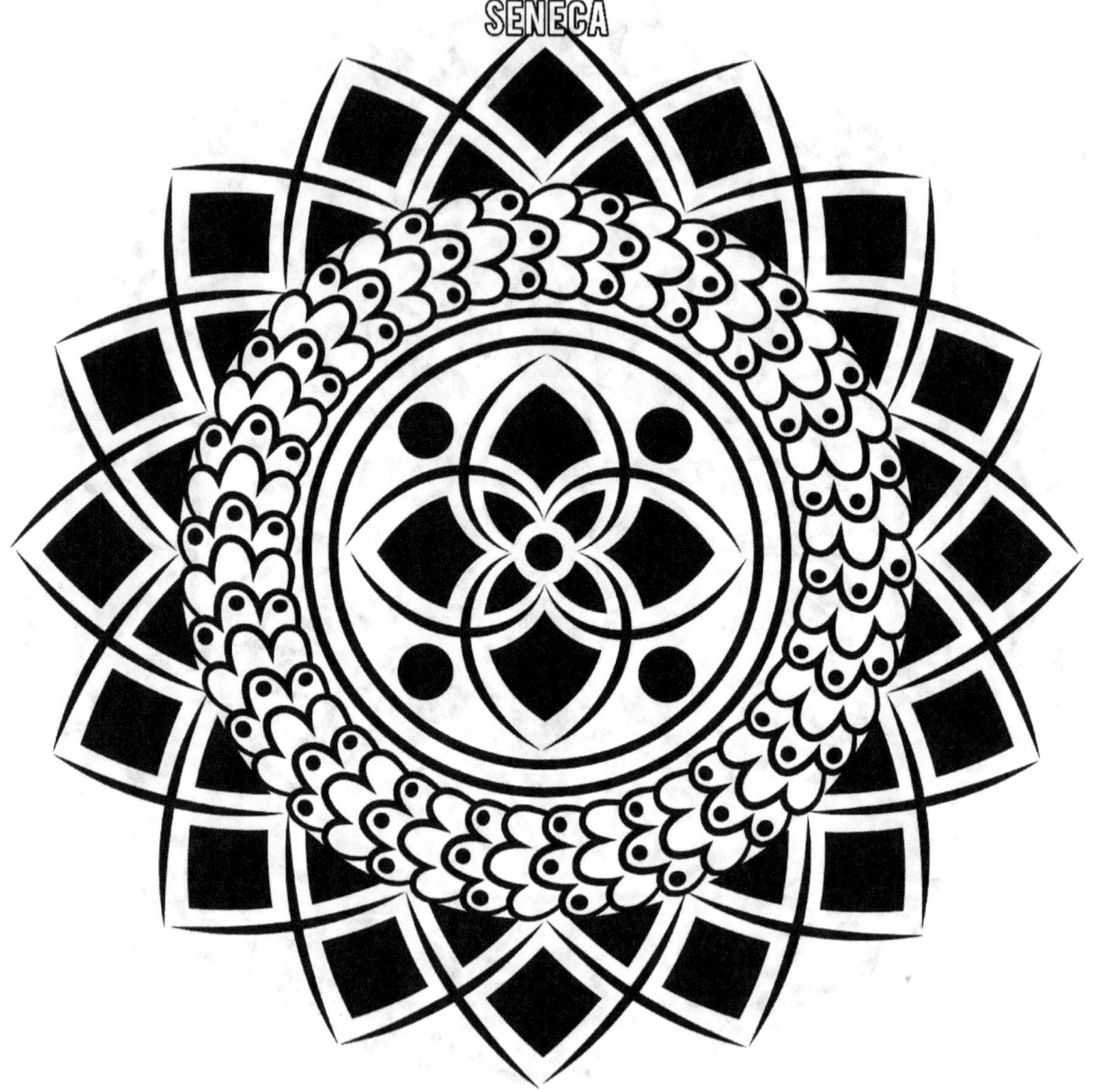

"THE FIRST STEP TOWARDS GETTING SOMEWHERE
IS TO DECIDE
THAT YOU ARE NOT GOING TO STAY WHERE YOU ARE."
JOHN PIERPONT MORGAN

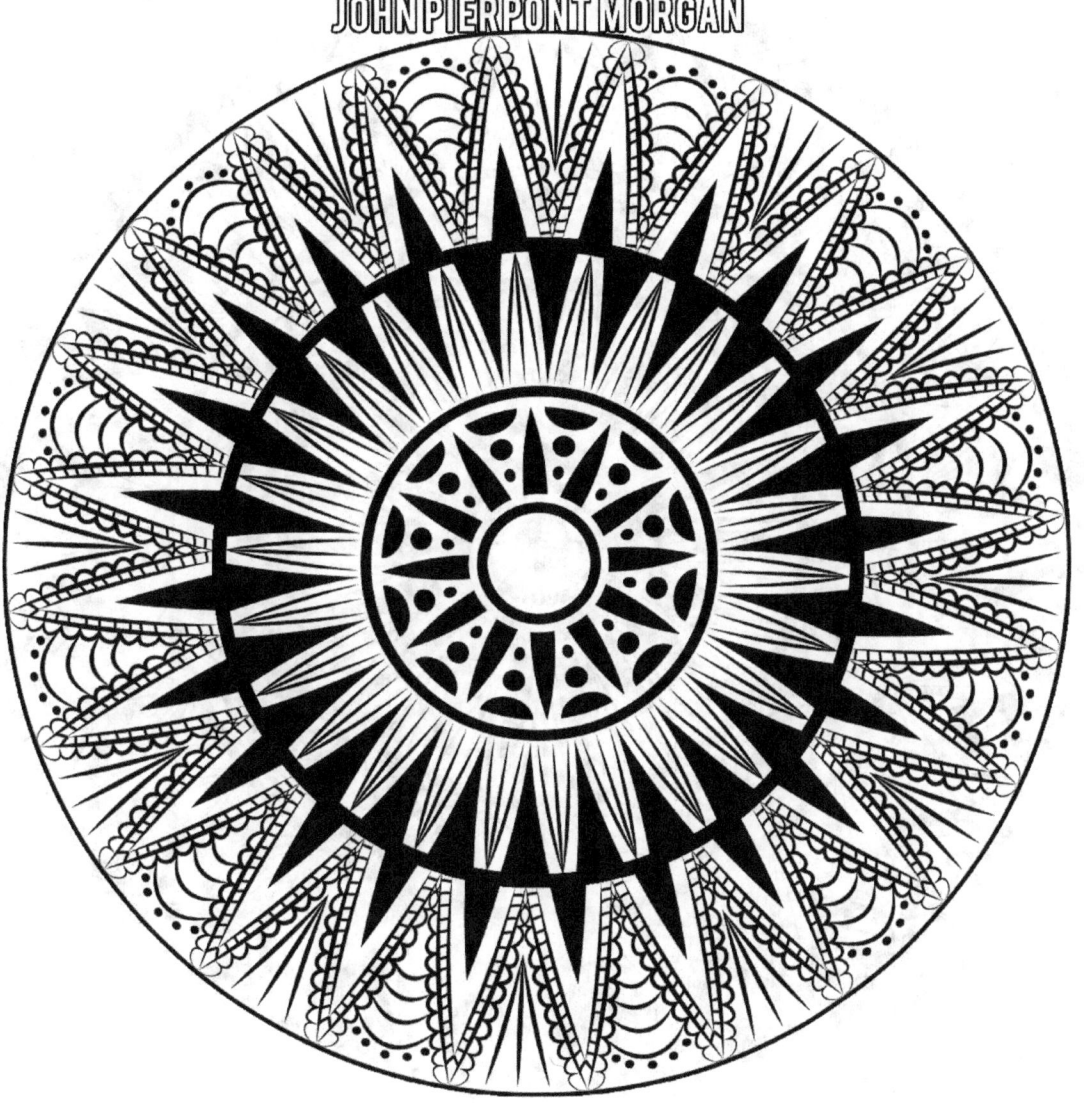

"GREATNESS DOES NOT APPROACH HIM
WHO IS FOREVER LOOKING DOWN."
HITOPADESA

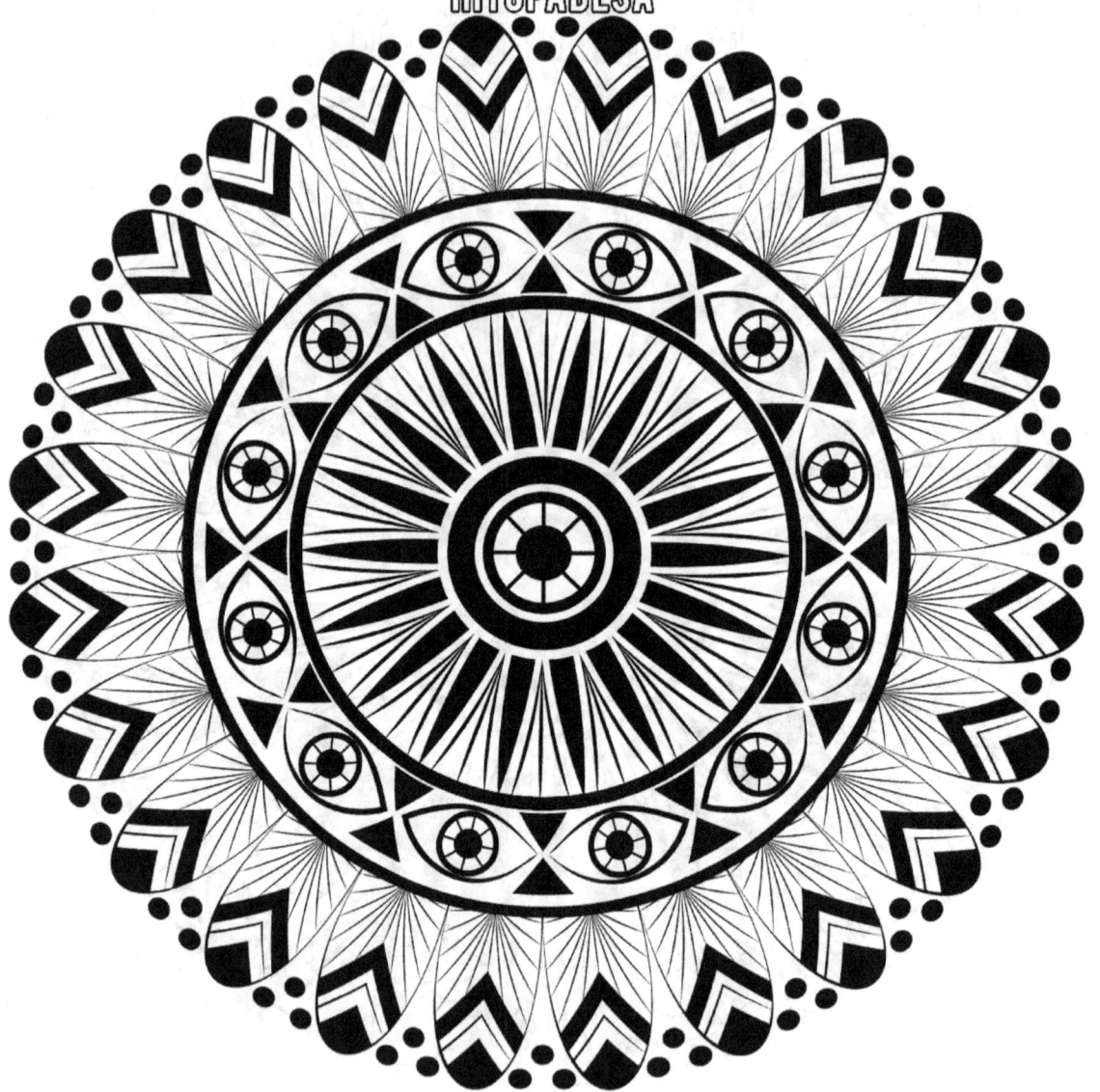

"HAPPINESS COMES OF THE CAPACITY TO FEEL DEEPLY,
TO ENJOY SIMPLY, TO THINK FREELY,
TO RISK LIFE, TO BE NEEDED."
S. JAMESON

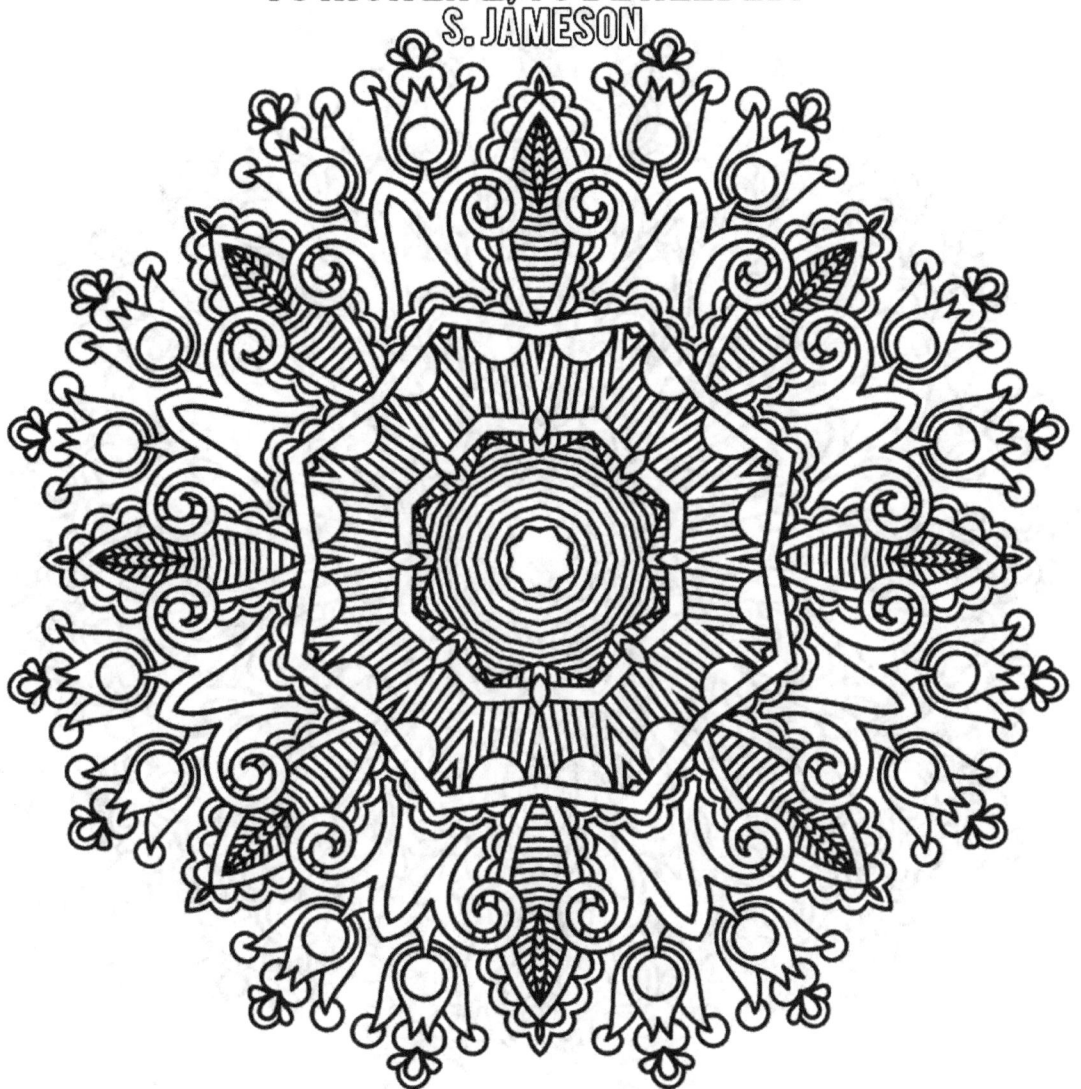

"SPEAK CLEARLY, IF YOU SPEAK AT ALL;
CARVE EVERY WORD BEFORE YOU LET IT FALL."
OLIVER WENDELL HOLMES

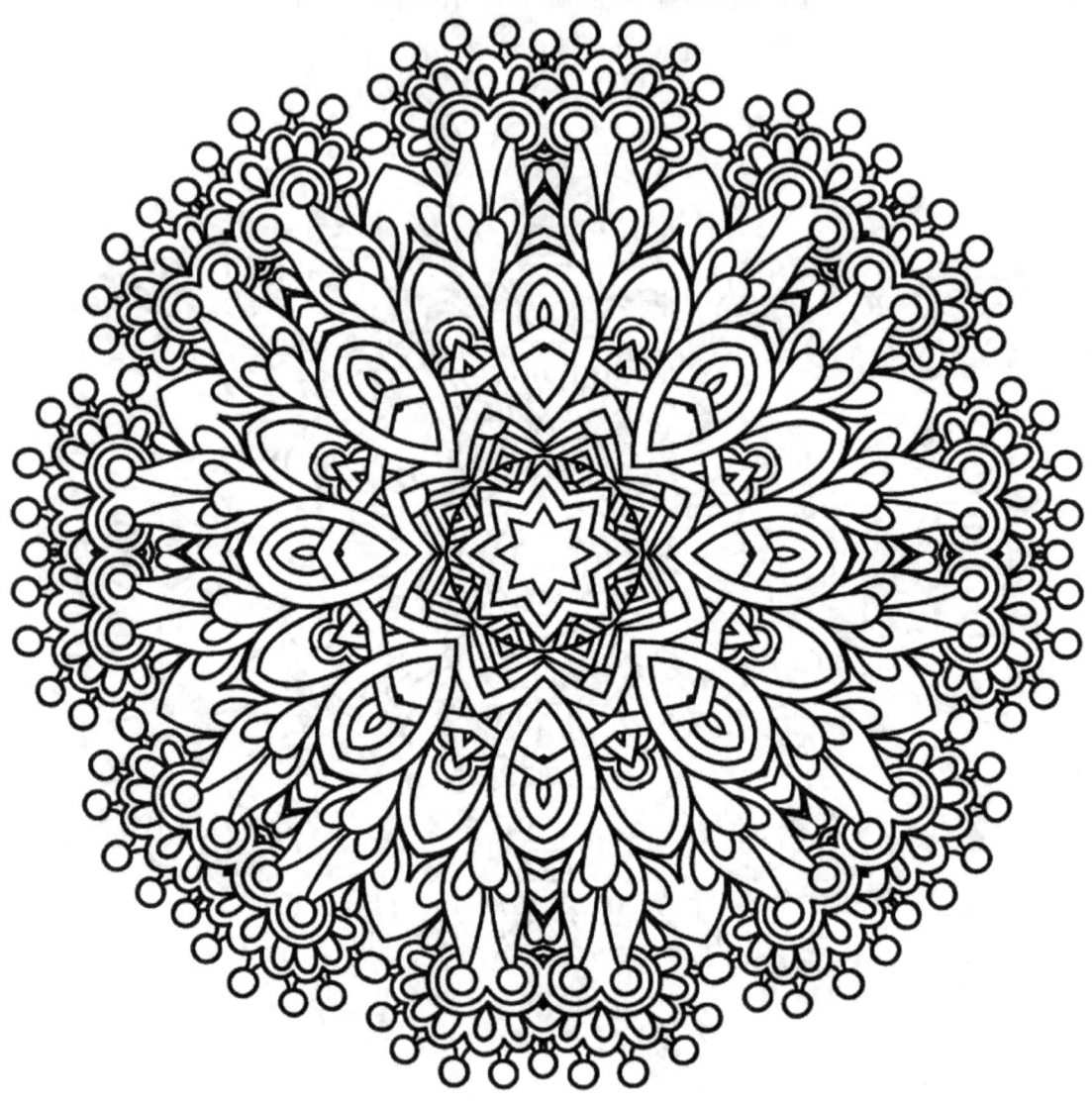

"HIDE NOT YOUR TALENTS. THEY FOR USE WERE MADE.
WHAT'S A SUNDIAL IN THE SHADE?"
BENJAMIN FRANKLIN

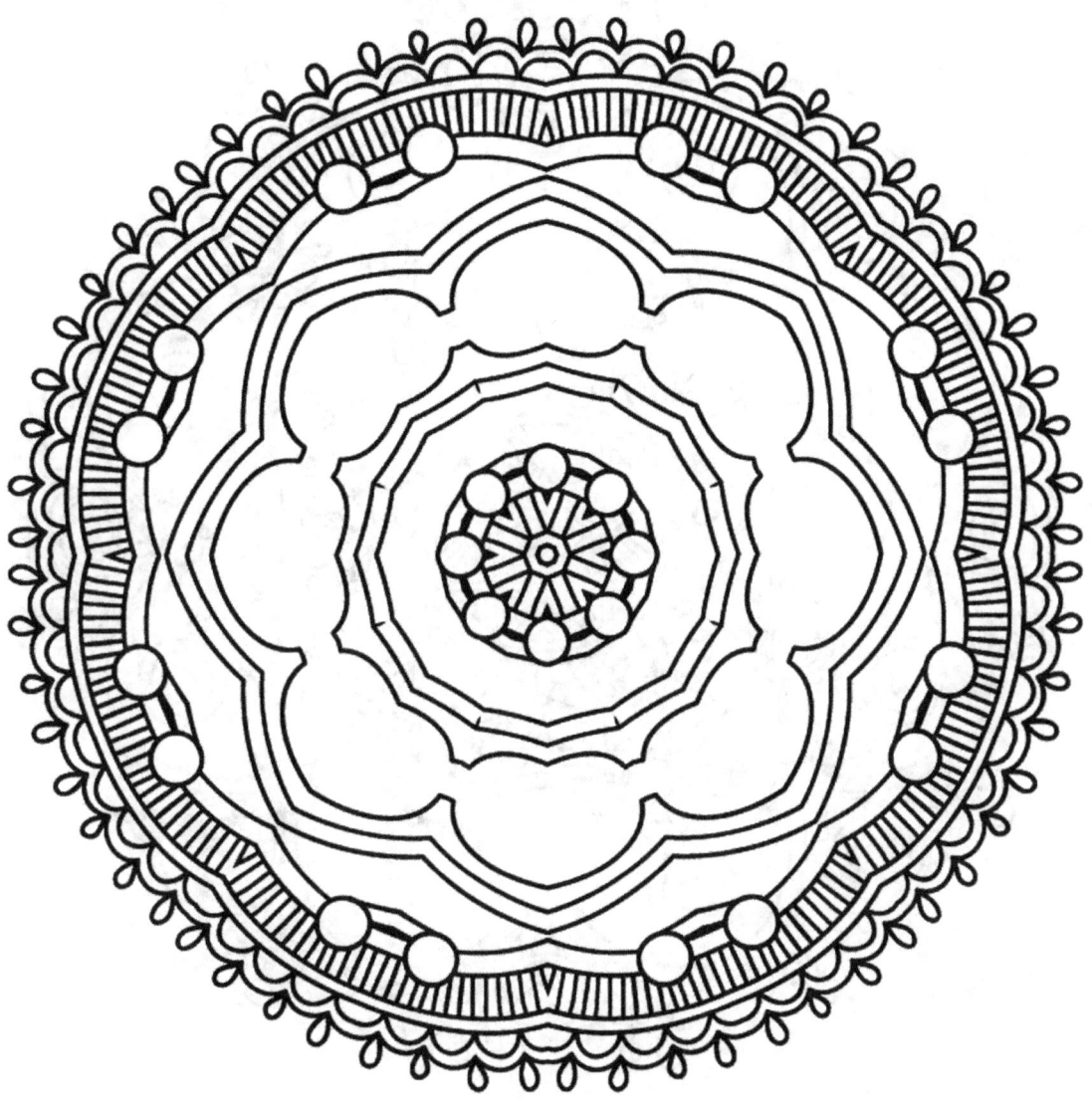

"SPOON FEEDING IN THE LONG RUN
TEACHES US NOTHING BUT THE SHAPE OF THE SPOON."
E. M. FORSTER

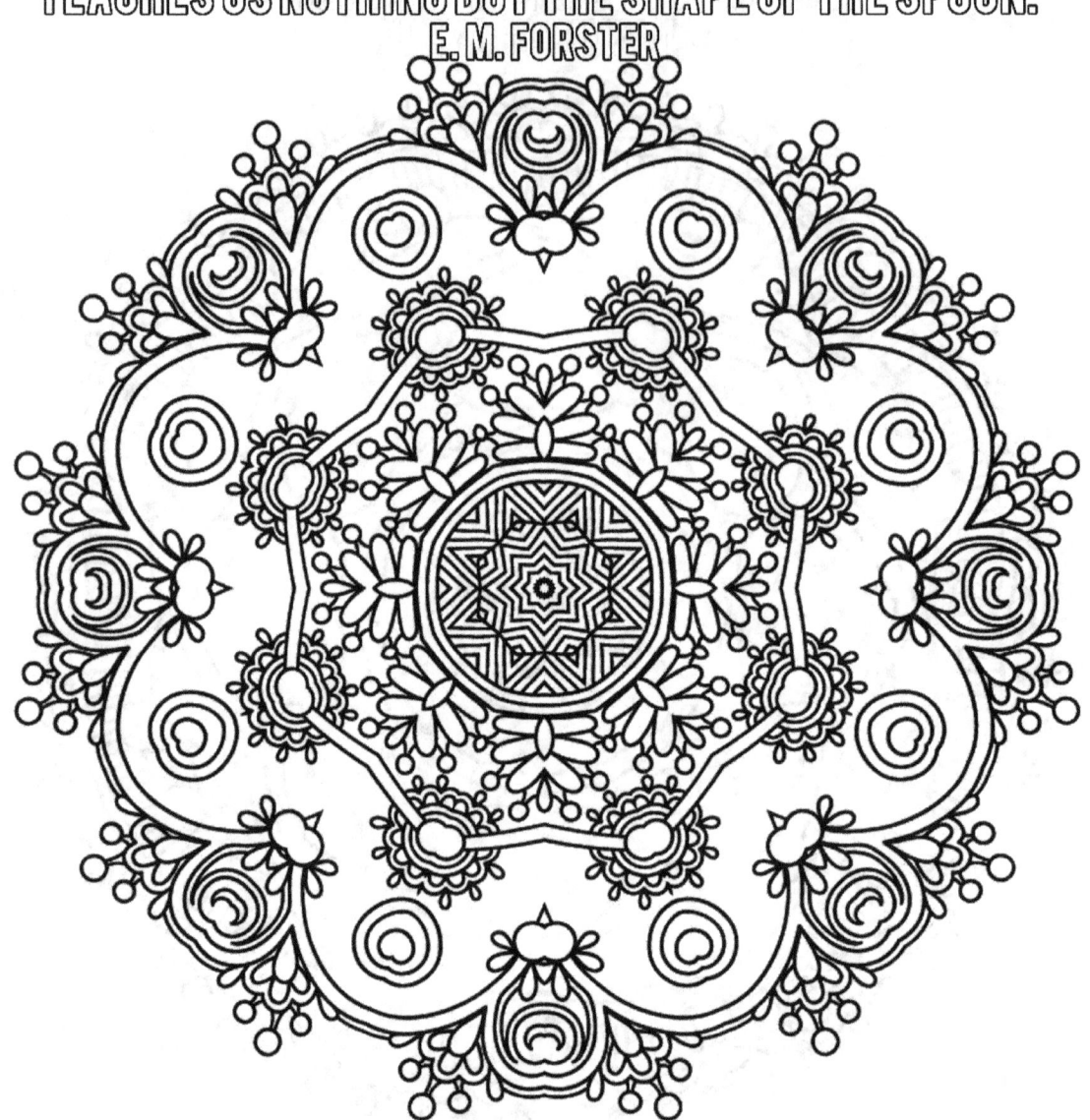

"ACTION IS ELOQUENCE."
WILLIAM SHAKESPEARE

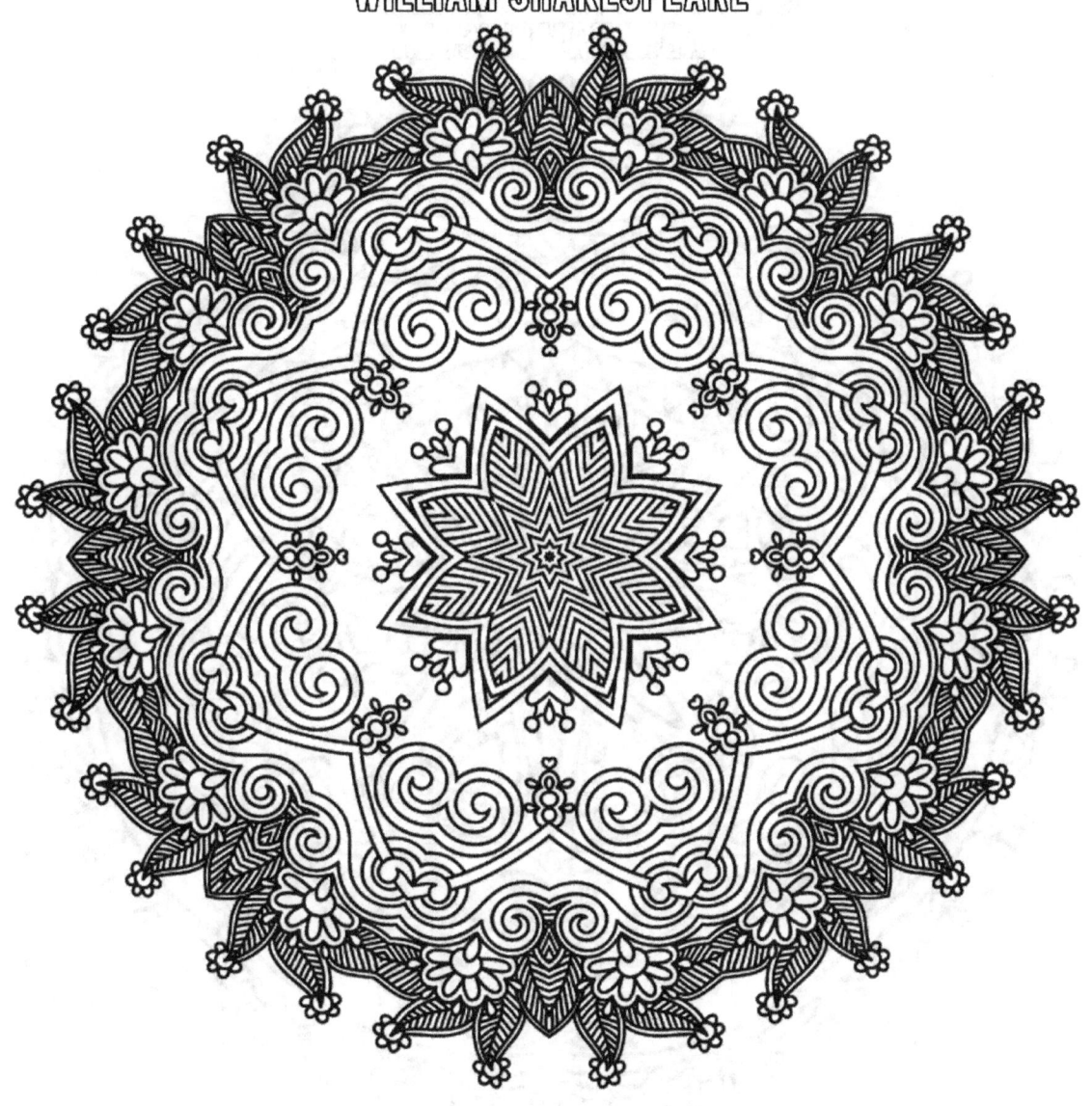

"I DON'T LIKE THAT MAN.
I MUST GET TO KNOW HIM BETTER."
ABRAHAM LINCOLN

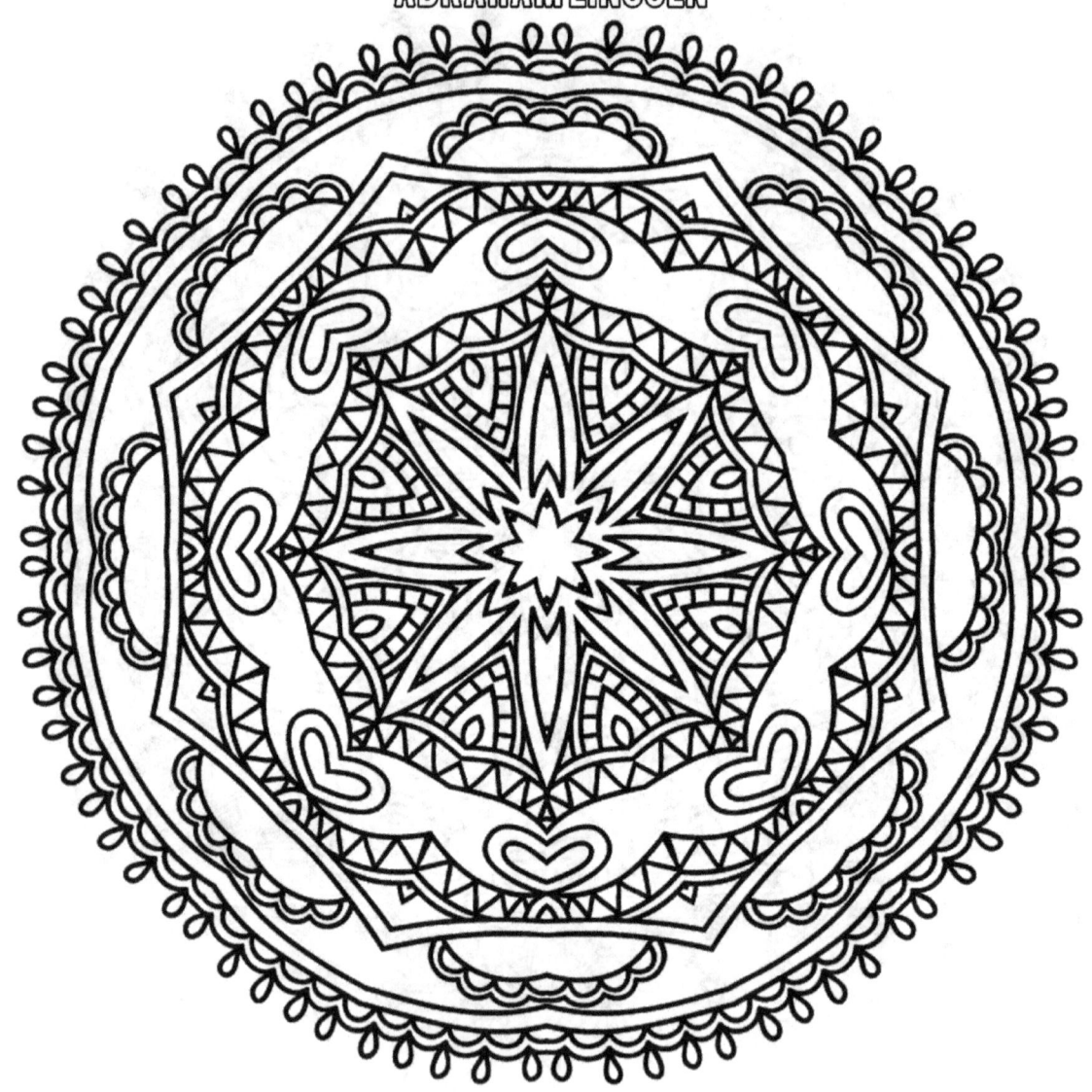

"THERE IS ONLY ONE SUCCESS,
TO BE ABLE TO SPEND YOUR LIFE IN YOUR OWN WAY."
CHRISTOPHER MORLEY

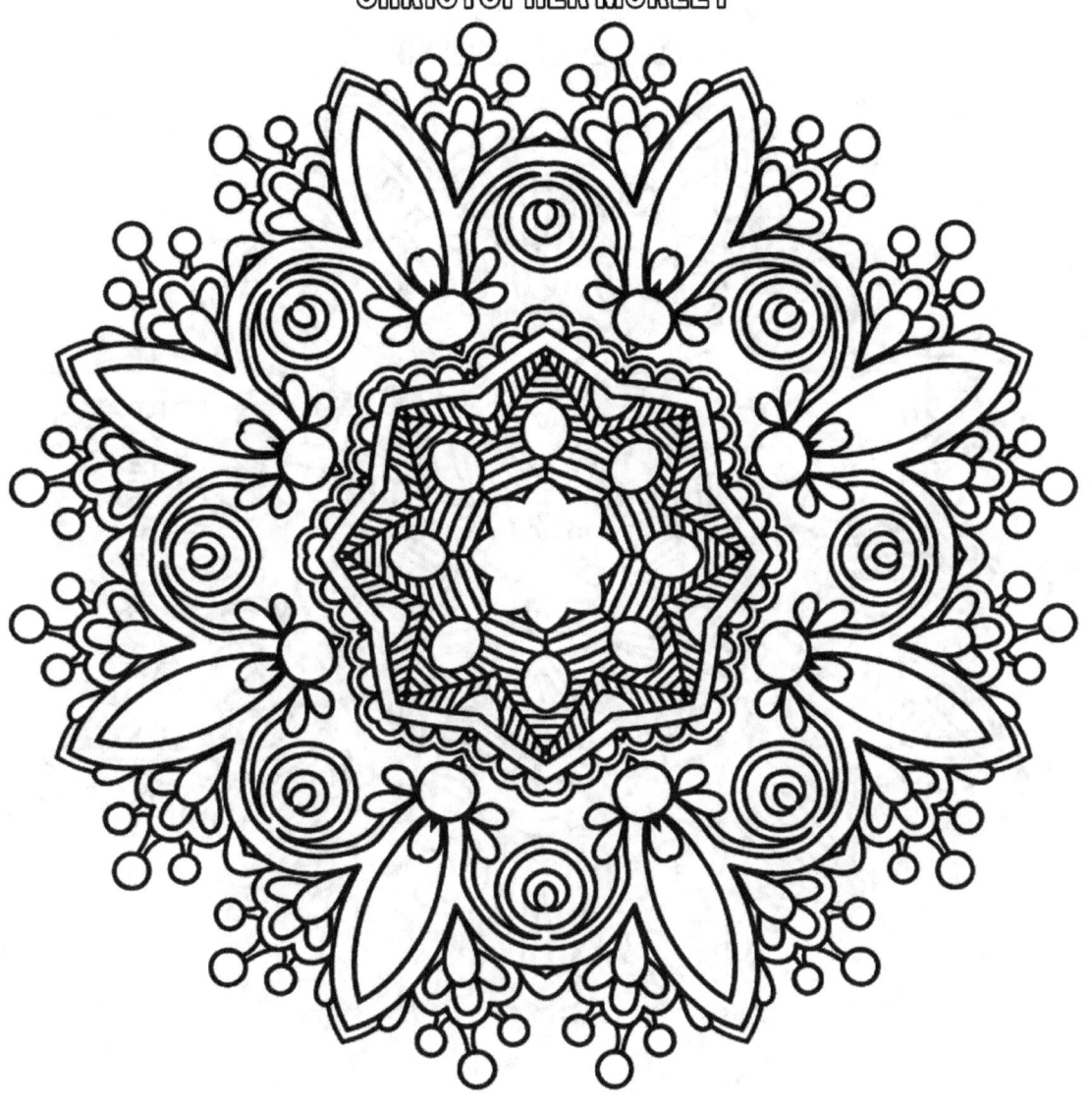

"YOU SEE THINGS; AND YOU SAY 'WHY?'
BUT I DREAM THINGS THAT NEVER WERE;
AND I SAY 'WHY NOT?'"
GEORGE BERNARD SHAW

101 INSPIRATIONAL COLORING MANDALAS
Curated by Todd Cotton

If you enjoyed this book, you can learn more about our ever-growing library of books and products (*or even join the club for substantial discounts!*) at:
http://www.101bookclub.com/

Please like us on Facebook at:
https://www.facebook.com/101BookClubTeam/

If you have questions or ideas for new books or products for your 101 Book Club Library, contact us via email at *info@101bookclub.com*!

Best wishes in your future endeavors!

Respectfully,

Todd Cotton

If you enjoyed this book, we think you will LOVE our 101 Bible Heroes Coloring Book! Check it out at *http://www.101bookclub.com/* .

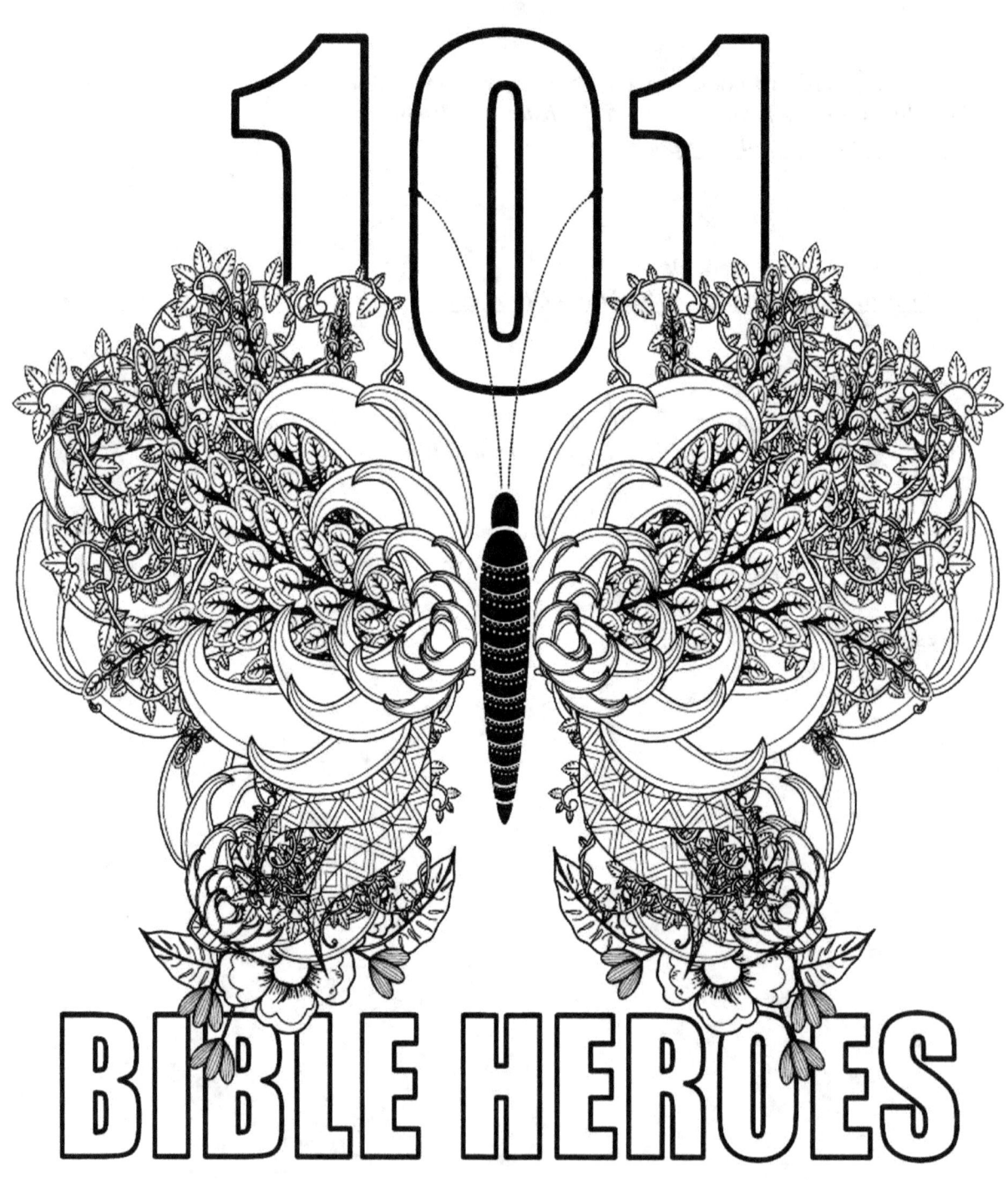

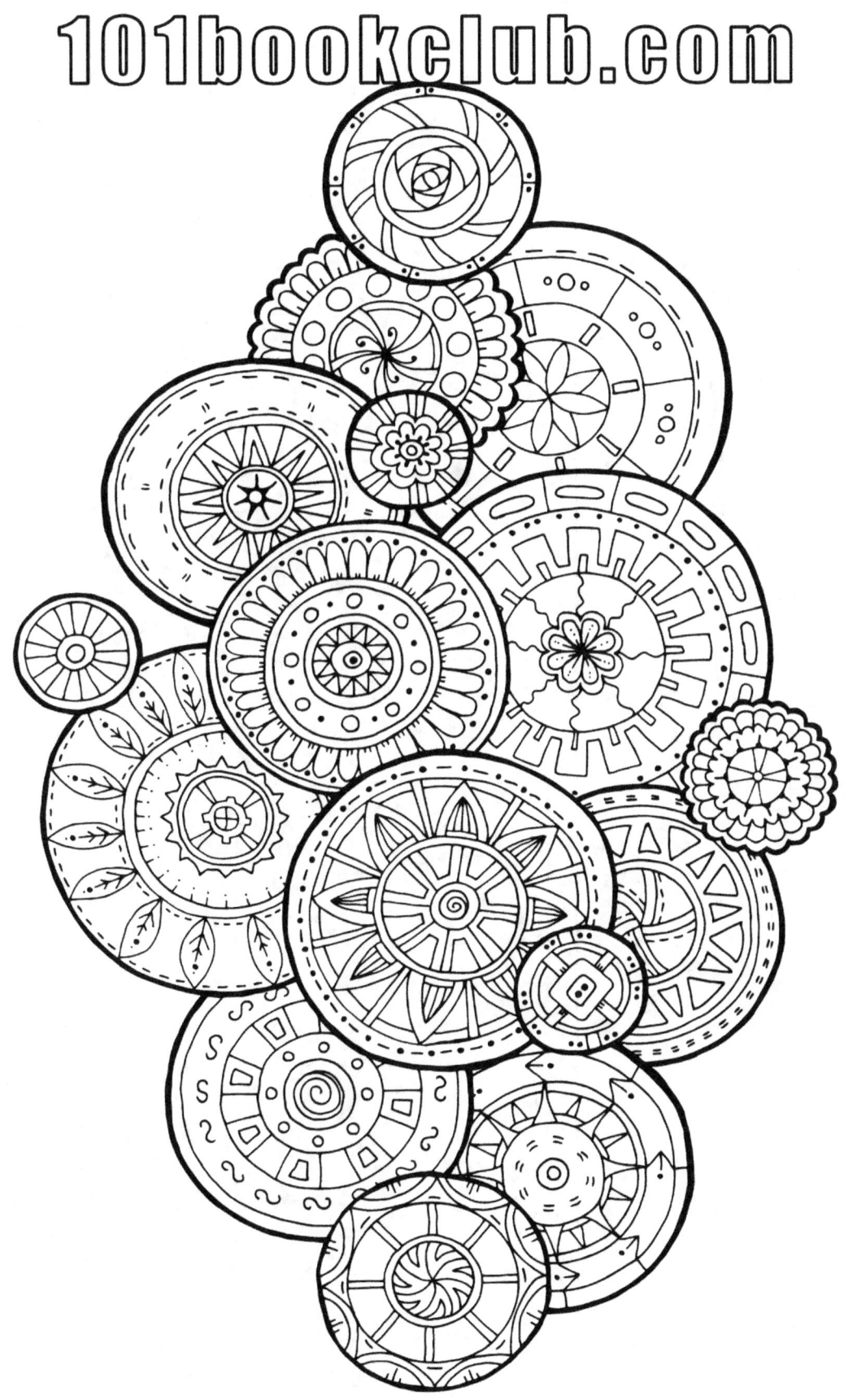